Little Laureates

London & The Home Counties
Edited by Heather Killingray

Young Writers

First published in Great Britain in 2007 by:
Young Writers
Remus House
Coltsfoot Drive
Peterborough
PE2 9JX
Telephone: 01733 890066
Website: www.youngwriters.co.uk

All Rights Reserved

© Copyright Contributors 2007

SB ISBN 978-1 84602 914 1

Foreword

Young Writers was established in 1991 and has been passionately devoted to the promotion of reading and writing in children and young adults ever since. The quest continues today. Young Writers remains as committed to the nurturing of poetic and literary talent as ever.

This year's Young Writers competition has proven as vibrant and dynamic as ever and we are delighted to present a showcase of the best poetry from across the UK and in some cases overseas. Each poem has been selected from a wealth of *Little Laureates* entries before ultimately being published in this, our sixteenth primary school poetry series.

Once again, we have been supremely impressed by the overall quality of the entries we have received. The imagination, energy and creativity which has gone into each young writer's entry made choosing the poems a challenging and often difficult but ultimately hugely rewarding task - the general high standard of the work submitted ensured this opportunity to bring their poetry to a larger appreciative audience.

We sincerely hope you are pleased with this final collection and that you will enjoy *Little Laureates London & The Home Counties* for many years to come.

Contents

All Saints' CE Primary School, Carshalton
    Timothy Cheng (8)   1

Brockham School, Brockham
    Polly Jordan (9)   1
    Amelia Schmitt (9)   2
    Lili Phillips (8)   2
    Laura Amos (8)   3
    Jemima Leney (8)   3
    Caroline Aylin Watson (8)   4
    Miles Cresswell (8)   4
    Suzanne Parish (9)   5
    Joshua Parker (8)   5

Capel Primary School, Tonbridge
    Chloe Lauren Franklin (11)   6
    Monique Foulger (11)   6
    Toby Loveday (10)   7
    William Baker (10)   7
    George McLaggan (10)   8
    Jade Louise Vincent   8
    William Melhuish (10)   9
    Emma Knowles (10)   9
    Emily Louise Ellis (10)   10
    Francesca Andrews (10)   10
    Maisy Edwards (11)   11
    Daniel Lawson (11)   11
    Ryan Baker (10)   12
    James Miller   12
    Christopher Eldred (10)   13
    Charlie Bottger (10)   13
    Kelly Phillips   14
    Christie Mann (11)   14
    Dominic Baker (11)   15
    Danielle Nicole Turner   15
    Jake Cheesman (11)   16
    Sophie Louise Roffe (11)   16
    Joshua Wells (11)   17

Monty Daly (10)	17
Ella Marie Hambly (10)	18
Jack Floyd-Latham (10)	18
Jacob Henry Wise (10)	19

Charlton CE Primary School, Dover
Sophie Parfitt (8)	19
Nathan Locke (8)	19
Beatrice Vaughan (9)	20
Nicole Larke (9)	20
Matthew Cragg (8)	21
Vikki Uden (9)	21
Isabel Lily Marples (8)	22
Sean Knight (9)	22
Jasmine Alice Kember (8)	22
Jake Smissen (9)	23

Cleves School, Weybridge
Charlotte Brooke-Pearce (7)	23
Gaby Gleeson (8)	24
Sophie Denham (8)	24
Sally Hoyle (7)	25
Robyn Edwards (7)	25

Edge Grove School, Aldenham Village
Alexander Cook (9)	26
Oreoluwa Olubode (7)	27
Ned Holland-Hibbert (7)	28
James Nutt (7)	29
Harvey Presence (9)	29
Rohit Biswas (7)	30

Four Elms Primary School, Edenbridge
Amy Edmeads (9)	31
Aaron Freeman (7) & Sam Moseley (8)	31
Luke Burns (9) & Patrick Collier (8)	31
Sarah Partridge (9)	32
Samantha Tilley (7)	32
Mollie Longhurst (7)	33
Emily Longhurst (6)	33

Isobel Money (7)	34
Zoe Priston (8)	34
Hope Fuller (8)	35
Milly Money (7)	36
Melody Bicknell (7)	36
Caitlin Kickham (9) & Michaela Haynes (8)	37
Andrew Gledhill-Carr (11)	37
Aston Bradshaw (11)	38

Kingsnorth CE Primary School, Ashford

David Whitford (9)	38
Dominic Osborne (9)	38
Maisey Twomey (10)	38
Richard Phillip Wilson (9)	39
Ashleigh Ann Wheal (9)	39
Farid White (9)	40
Emily Joy Harris (10)	40
Will Flockett (9)	41
Natasha Francis (10)	41
Joanne Sheppard (9)	42
William Ashdown (9)	42
Orla McGlone (9)	43
Molly McKeown (9)	43
Ben Harte (9)	44
George Paul (10)	44
Martin Nichols (10)	45
Kayleigh Winn (9)	45
Jamie Nichols (10)	46
Amber Court (9)	46
Jack Sims (10), Callum Booth & Dan Bottachi (9)	47
Eleanor Denniss (10)	47

Larkrise Primary School, Chelmsford

Danny Theobald (10)	48
Jordan Northrop (10)	48
Ben Howard (11)	48
Marnie Bevan (11)	49
Jessica Hubbard (10)	49
Kimberley Brewster (11)	50
Lewis Hilden (11)	50
Bryoni Dale (11)	51

Ashleigh Sinden (10)   51
Nathan Watkinson (11)   52
Shaun Evans (10)   52
Harry Charlick (10)   53
Christie Schott (10)   53

Monega Primary School, London
Chahat Shah (11)   54
Isabel Fanfan (11)   54
Junaid Mahmood (10)   55
Tasnima Khanom (11)   55
Rima Akthar (11)   56
Etse Umole (9)   56
Ayesha Vali (11)   57
Iqra Ali (10)   58
Nalisha Arya (9)   58
Dylan Dhinsa (9)   59
Sumayyah Shabbir (10)   59
Nazima Naznin (10)   60
Jasmin Begum (11)   60
Roshni Arya (11)   61
Zakiyah Begum (11)   61

Newlands Primary School, Ramsgate
Chloe Vissers (10)   62
Jonathan Moore (10)   62
Jayde Storey (10)   62
Sophie Allen (10)   63
Ellie Simpson (11)   63
Samuel Clark (11)   63
Zak Cohen (10)   64
Jack Warner (11)   64
Sean Fairhurst (11)   65
Jarrett Francis (11)   65
Anastasia Batten (10)   65
Sian Hayes (11)   66
Limar Atiera (10)   66
Megan Brown (11)   66
Conor Hope (11)   67
Hanna Bowley (10)   67
Gabrielle Challis (8)   67

Siâna Smith (11)	68
Rachel Adkins (8)	68
Katherine Stirrups (7)	68
Kye Boughton (8)	69
Olivia Turner (7)	69
Kieran Horsley (8)	69
Darcey Bennett (8)	70
Christian Pressagh (8)	70
Vickie Vizer (8)	70
Jack Hanes-Callis (8)	71
Harley Jones (7)	71
Tilly Shakeshaft (8)	71
Jack Burnap (7)	72

Oakfield School, Pyrford
Philippa Helen Rooney (11)	72

Our Lady of Lourdes RC Primary School, London
Chinazo Orji (9)	73

Radwinter CE Primary School, Saffron Walden
Anna Midgley (10)	73
Ivan Karsten (11)	74
Alice Moore (11)	74
Max Clay (11)	75
Victoria Vicary (10)	75
Thea Rudder Logan (10)	76
Rhys Basham (11)	76
Jack Mitchison (10)	77
Eve Hillier-Clarke (11)	77
Sam Larlham (10)	78
Terry Duck (11)	78
Dominic Byrne (11)	79
Aidan Clarke (11)	79
Florrie Priest (11)	80
Michael Coe (11)	81

Sandcross School, Reigate
Harriet Wood (8)	81
Emma Elson (10)	82

Megan Smith (10)	83
Ellie Christie (10)	84
Gemma Cathie (9)	85
Mark Reynolds (9)	86
Alex Chowne (9)	87
Clodagh Wells (8)	88
Jonathan Day (9)	88
Megan Bailey (10)	89
Eleanor Riches (8)	90

Scargill Junior School, Rainham
Abbie Taylor (9)	90

Sibertswold CE Primary School, Dover
Claire Penny (10)	91
Annabel Reville (11)	91
Sarah Penny (10)	92
Jacob Roberts (10)	92
Shannah Hall (11)	93
Laura Palmer (11)	93
Brandon Forrest (10)	94
Hannah Coupe (10)	94

Temple Hill CP School, Dartford
Stephanie Homewood (10)	95
Tyler Tanner (9)	95
Alfie Day (9)	96
Harry Ring (10)	97
William Azeza (10)	98
Billy Troke (10)	98
Laura Maxwell (9)	99
Shannon Burkley (10)	100
Orla Taylor (9)	102
Liam Ward (10)	103
Callum Smith (9)	104
Rachel Massen (9)	105
Cynthia Ndungu (9)	106

Whitstable Endowed CE (A) Junior School, Whitstable
Jevan Rowe (9)	106

Maddy Perry (9) 106
Richard Rowland (9) 107
William Goldsworthy (9) 107
Joseph Thundow (10) 108
Michael Thundow (10) 109
Oliver Ingham (9) 109
Lauren Abbott (10) 110
Hollie Pring (9) 110
Amber Manning (11) 111
Maddy Temple (9) 111
Andy Beaumont (10) 112
Katie Horton (11) 113
Katy Terrell (11) 113
Eleanor Dwyers (10) 114

Yerbury Primary School, London
Thomas Dwyer (9) 114

The Poems

Thomas Green

Thomas Green
Thomas Green
Went into the room with the washing machine

Thomas Green
Thomas Green
Stuck his head in a rushing machine

Rushing machine
Washing machine
Round and round Thomas Green

Thomas Green
Thomas Green
Cleanest kid the world's ever seen

Ever seen
Thomas Green
Put his head in a rushing machine

Thomas Green
Thomas Green
Cleanest ghost I've ever seen!

Timothy Cheng (8)
All Saints' CE Primary School, Carshalton

Winter's Day

W hirling snow softly falls
 I cicles hang tightly on walls
N ature hides in the snowy branches
T wisting snowballs hit people with dances
E legant snowflakes slowly drop
R ipe fruits are ready to pop
S ilent wind blows off hats

D rifting snow goes by cats
A ll the snowmen are amazing and stunning
Y oung children always running.

Polly Jordan (9)
Brockham School, Brockham

Rim Of Heaven

R ed robins singing aloud
I vy vines hanging down
M ysterious cat creeping about

O n the top of a mountain lies a luxury place, are you ready to climb
F lowing stream, heads eastward toward the sea

H eavenly gardens filled with silence
E ver beauty across the land
A s the stag emerges from the temple, wild animals gather round
V iew divine, glittering lake, fish swimming about
E nd of light is due as the moon rises
N o sound is here, but peace.

Amelia Schmitt (9)
Brockham School, Brockham

I Dream

I dream of being a fairy
And hair with lots of curls,
A beautiful sparkling dress,
To match my glittering pearls.

Shoes made of crystal,
Earrings made of gold,
Fingertips painted
And a lovely wand to hold.

My eyes are sparkling blue,
My cheeks are rosy red,
My lips are very pink
And now it's time for bed.

I love to dream,
I love to dream,
Laying on my satin wings.

Lili Phillips (8)
Brockham School, Brockham

Teddy

My teddy is very pretty,
She wears a velvety dress,
But I think she is very fussy,
Because she only eats cress.

My teddy went to school with me
And broke the school rules with me,
But when the teacher told me off,
I said it was my teddy.

At school at lunch, teddy came with me
And asked for potato and tomato,
But then she was sick,
But she still had a lick of my lolly on a stick.

When we got home,
We were sent to beddy, beddy, beddy
And all I could say
Was goodnight teddy!

Laura Amos (8)
Brockham School, Brockham

Winter's Day

W oolly socks and a fire
I cicles scattering on the ground
N early school again
T wittering robins calling for summer
E gg on toast for tea
R ound, round go the skaters on the ice rink
S now slowly landing on roads

D own comes the powerful snow
A way in the Manger sing the carollers
Y ellow hat and scarves on a cold little child.

Jemima Leney (8)
Brockham School, Brockham

Winter's Night

W inter so cold and frosty
I cicles hanging from the top of windowpanes
N ight so dark and moonlit
T he owls swoop down looking for prey
E legantly past comes the smallest, tiniest snowflake
R obins making tiny footprints on the tree branches
S nowflakes falling down like rain

N ight so peaceful and quiet with animals hibernating everywhere
I ce surrounding the fish pond, freezing it, making it an ice ring
G ardens covered in a white blanket of snow
H igh trees with snow on branches, red berries on the tree
T insel being thrown onto trees, making them beautiful.

Caroline Aylin Watson (8)
Brockham School, Brockham

Winter's Day

W hite world covered with sparkling snow
I cicles hanging from the bare trees
N ew snow from dark clouds
T riumphant dogs nosing around in the snow
E ating roast turkey
R ed robin, red breast, sitting in a red nest
S tanding in the deep snow

D elivering the daily news
A t 2.00 in the afternoon, we open presents
Y ippee! We get to stay up late, I hope I see you soon.

Miles Cresswell (8)
Brockham School, Brockham

My Dream World

My dream world is a great place
When love and friendship is no race
A beautiful light blue sky
And a happy life until we die.

The grass is silky and green
No one around is mean
The sun is shining mile to mile
And everyone with a beaming smile.

The joy of a cold, winter's day
The clean, white snow on the ground it lay
Children's laughter in the air
Playing nicely without a care.

People lying on the beach
And all the anger out of reach
As the frothy sea goes in and out
Making crashing noises like a shout.

This is my world of dreams!

Suzanne Parish (9)
Brockham School, Brockham

Winter's Day

W intry wind blowing snow into drifts
I cicles hanging from dark, frosty roofs
N ippy wind like somebody punching you
T he children are throwing snowballs
E xcited children shouting
R apid snow falling down
S nowflakes dropping slowly

D ark and frosty night
A nimals plodding through the snow
Y oung children making a snowman.

Joshua Parker (8)
Brockham School, Brockham

The Blitz

The Blitz
Always demolishing buildings,
Ear-splitting, resounding, thundering,
Like huge cymbals booming together,
Like a huge blanket full of bombs,
I feel frightened, terrified in fact,
I feel like my life is over in just one minute,
The Blitz
Reminds me how precious life really is.

The Blitz
Destroying anything in sight,
Thunderous, deafening, shrieking,
Like a death door approaching,
Like it's me they want to kill,
I feel worried, petrified,
The Blitz
Reminds us how lucky we all really are.

Chloe Lauren Franklin (11)
Capel Primary School, Tonbridge

The Blitz

The bombing blitz
Bombs destroying everything in sight
Crashes, bangs, cries
The Blitz, as violent as an attacking dog
Blitz as ferocious as a shark
I feel scared, worried
The bombing blitz
It makes me feel how short life really is.

Monique Foulger (11)
Capel Primary School, Tonbridge

The Booming Blitz

The booming blitz
It terrifies everyone!
Loud, clashing, destructive,
Like a million machine guns on auto-shoot,
Like a nuclear bomb exploding everywhere,
It makes me feel appreciative
And glad I am safe
The booming blitz
Reminds us of how lucky we really are.

The exploding World War II
Hitler v Churchill,
Booming, explosions, 1939 to 1945,
Like a cacophony of crashes,
Like a thousand grenades got set off at the same time,
As scared as a small puppy,
Like a cockroach getting crushed,
The exploding World War II
It makes me feel scared and terrified.

Toby Loveday (10)
Capel Primary School, Tonbridge

World War II

The smell of the planes' propellers
Is like sewage and death.
The sound is like thunder
And water crashing together.
It looks like horrific
Fire surrounding them.
I feel like I am sinking into
The deep blue sea.
World War II
It covers the world with danger.

William Baker (10)
Capel Primary School, Tonbridge

The Blazing Blitz

The blazing blitz
Planes soaring through the air
Clattering, crashing, a cacophony of noises
Like Hell
As terrifying as a shark coming towards me
Petrified, terrified, mortified
I'm trembling like a frightened puppy
The blazing blitz
Reminds me of how short life is.

The blitzing bombs
Dropping from all angles
Blazing, obliterating, devastating
Like death in a ball
Like an avalanche
It's breathtaking
Like devastation coming out of a plane
The blitzing bombs
Reminds us of how precious life is.

George McLaggan (10)
Capel Primary School, Tonbridge

The Bombing Backlash!

The bombing backlash
The bomb falls, the siren calls
Intimidating, demolishing, destructive
Like a malicious man destroying all
Like a dark shadow creeping towards us in the moonlit sky
I feel worried, petrified and nervous
Like a fly stranded in the vast sky
Reminds us that some people's lives have been cut short
The bombing backlash.

Jade Louise Vincent
Capel Primary School, Tonbridge

The Bulging Blitz

The bulging blitz
A cacophony of noises
Deadly, destructive, devastating
Like a never-ending life
Like Hell itself is here
It makes me feel petrified
Like a statue standing coldly still
The bulging blitz
It reminds me of how painful life can be.

World War II
Countries fighting
Scared, nervous, terrified
Like a gun destroying lives
Like the decision of life and death
I feel like I've got a new sense of danger
Like a mouse running for cover
World War II
It reminds me of a friendship between countries.

William Melhuish (10)
Capel Primary School, Tonbridge

The Blitz

The deadly Blitz
Hundreds of people
Dying each second
Deafening, booming, malicious
Like a catapult hung in the sky
Like a loud orchestra
Playing at full blast
It makes me feel helpless
Like a prisoner in jail
The Blitz, the deadly Blitz
Reminds me of how violent the world can be.

Emma Knowles (10)
Capel Primary School, Tonbridge

Wicked World War II

Blackout Blitz
Bombs fall over the blacked-out house
Dingy, dismal, dismay!
Like a million black moons
Falling onto the black sky
Like a night with no day
I feel like the gasses floating nowhere
Like a star stranded on a black canvas
Blackout Blitz
Reminds us what life used to be like.

Concentration camps
Full of unfortunate Jews
Disappointment, frustration, helplessness
Annoying like a crying baby
Destroying for everyone's heart
I feel terrible for those Jews
I feel so upset like a mother
Who has lost her child
Concentration camps
Reminds us how disgusting Hitler was.

Emily Louise Ellis (10)
Capel Primary School, Tonbridge

Blackout Blitz

Blackout Blitz
Terrible tormenting deaths
Dangerous, devastating, distressing
As dark as the night sky at midnight
I see one of the German's last flights
I feel scared, cold and dingy
I feel as lonely, dull and dark
As a tree silhouette in the middle of a field
Blackout Blitz
Remember the day when all was dark and lonesome.

Francesca Andrews (10)
Capel Primary School, Tonbridge

The Blazing Blitz

The Blazing Blitz
Searchlights swinging everywhere
Rowdy, roaring raids
As terrifying as sharks' teeth
As haunting as a ghost
I sense danger in the air
Like a rhino thundering towards me
The Blazing Blitz
Reminds me how precious life is!

The demolishing bombs
Falling from great heights
Crashing, colossal, courage
As scary as a pointy-nosed witch
As spooky as a dark, dingy walkway
I want to be free
Free like a bird
The demolishing bombs
Remind me how short life can be!

Maisy Edwards (11)
Capel Primary School, Tonbridge

The Dreadful Blitz

Booming and screaming
The Blitz is terrible
The blackout has begun
A thousand bombs dropped from the moonlight sky
Spitfires protecting us in the misty sky
Flames cover London
The dreadful Blitz
Reminds me how lucky I really am.

Daniel Lawson (11)
Capel Primary School, Tonbridge

The Blitz

The Blitz
Is so dark
Dark, scary, malicious
As black as black paint
Malicious as a shark
It makes me feel scared
I feel as cold as an ice cube
The Blitz
A horrible day of death.

The planes
Bigger than an atomic bomb
Big, small, fast
Faster than a car
As fast as a jet
It makes me feel dead
I feel as scared as a vampire
The planes
A fast mode of transport.

Ryan Baker (10)
Capel Primary School, Tonbridge

The Blitz

The Blitz!

People always in the dark,
The smells hitting the atmosphere,
The army fighting for our country!

The blackout!

The bombs screeching when they hit the ground,
Children lost in the blackout!

James Miller
Capel Primary School, Tonbridge

World War II

World War II
Terrible, terrifying, bloodthirsty people,
Cacophony of carelessly crashing,
People petrified,
Screams and shouts from all around.
Buildings blowing up because of the horrible bombs,
Fluorescent fire furiously flaming,
People feel in danger, I feel so insecure,
Gunshots sound like glass smashing,
World War II
Makes people feel like it's the end of the world.

Christopher Eldred (10)
Capel Primary School, Tonbridge

The Blitz

The Blitz
It was a violent attack
Horrible, loud, deadly
Like a never-ending storm
Like a group of droning bees
I feel horrible
Like a drowning dog
The Blitz
Like a never-ending black tunnel.

Charlie Bottger (10)
Capel Primary School, Tonbridge

Blitz

World War Blitz
The Blitz dropping down on you
Banging, crashing, loud
Huge black blitz dropping
Like the blackout
Like a dog lost then . . .
I feel petrified of the black
When I'm all alone
World War Blitz
The world will not be the same.

Kelly Phillips
Capel Primary School, Tonbridge

The Blitz

The solemn Blitz
Made a terrifying cacophony of noises
Petrifying, deafening, dismal
Like a ghost clutching my throat
Like a prisoner in a rotting cell
It makes me feel nervously scared
It makes me feel alone and nobody cares
The solemn Blitz
Reminds us how heartbreaking life can be!

Christie Mann (11)
Capel Primary School, Tonbridge

The War

The vehicles of war
A plane
The jets reaching up into the air
Bombs, guns, dogfights
Like a boat sailing through a stormy sea
Like a bullet hitting some glass
It makes me feel lonely and timid
I feel like a shark swimming into a dark blue sea
A plane
Reminds me life is good.

Death in the garden
Britain in the Blitz
German planes hovering
Blackout, smacked out, get out!
Like a battle in space
Like a surprise of death
Lonely, small, cold
Like an ant in a cathedral
Britain in the Blitz
Reminds me that life can be kind.

Dominic Baker (11)
Capel Primary School, Tonbridge

World War II

People awaiting their death
Horrific, horrifying, horrid
As bad as the Earth coming to an end
Worse than a dragon burning everything in sight
I feel nervous that this might be my last day to live
I feel as bad as an army tank crushing everything
World War II
Makes me think this could be the end.

Danielle Nicole Turner
Capel Primary School, Tonbridge

The Phenomenal Blitz

People were petrified of the bombs
As they smashed into the cities
Terrified, scared and frightened people
The Blitz is so terrible
Bombs smashing through innocent people's houses
They must have felt frightened and scared
Because the next bomb might hit their house
The phenomenal Blitz
The worst nights ever in the blackout.

Jake Cheesman (11)
Capel Primary School, Tonbridge

The Blitz

The Blitz
Sixty-eight years ago
Scary, terrifying, disturbing
Like piercing thunder
Planes flying in the dark night
Like birds looking for their prey
It makes me feel concerned
Petrified as a bird when gunshots go off
The Blitz
Reminds us what the world is like.

Sophie Louise Roffe (11)
Capel Primary School, Tonbridge

The Enormous Blitz

The enormous Blitz
Like dashing thunder
Phenomenal, extraordinary, terrifying
As explosive as a bomb
Like fireworks in the night
It makes me feel as small as an ant
Like I am blind
The enormous Blitz
Reminds me of death.

Joshua Wells (11)
Capel Primary School, Tonbridge

The Blitz

The blazing Blitz,
Fluorescent searchlights beaming
Towards the jet-black sky,
Destructive, dingy and dreadful,
The crackling cacophony of gunshots,
I feel like a goldfish in a colossal aquarium,
I feel as lonely as a new kid at school,
The blazing Blitz,
Reminds us of how cruel life can be.

Monty Daly (10)
Capel Primary School, Tonbridge

The Terrifying Blitz

The terrifying Blitz
Outstanding, explosive, phenomenal
Disturbing, blazing flames
As bright as the yellow sun
Like a big scary firework display
Your heart being taken away
It makes me feel paralysed with fear
The terrifying Blitz
This was a frightening time.

Ella Marie Hambly (10)
Capel Primary School, Tonbridge

The Terrifying Blitz

The terrifying Blitz
1939 was when it started
Scary, noisy, disturbing
Like thunder all around
Like fire in the night
It makes me feel terrified like a trapped mouse
As petrified as a bird caught in the burning tree
The terrifying Blitz
It makes me frightened.

Jack Floyd-Latham (10)
Capel Primary School, Tonbridge

The Blitz

The Blitz
The booming bangs
Clashing, dangerous, loud
It's like cymbals clashing together
As loud as a lion's roaring
As scared as a little puppy
Like a tiny ant being crushed
The Blitz
It reminds me how safe we really are.

Jacob Henry Wise (10)
Capel Primary School, Tonbridge

Bouncing

Bouncing, bouncing,
Up high in the sky
Bouncing, bouncing,
If feels like you can fly!

Bouncing, bouncing,
Till you drop
Bouncing, bouncing,
Never stop!

Sophie Parfitt (8)
Charlton CE Primary School, Dover

Pets

My hamster and my rabbit
Are cuddly and sweet
They cuddle up together
And lick each other's feet.

Nathan Locke (8)
Charlton CE Primary School, Dover

Running

Run, run, *puff, puff,* up the hill I go,
Around the corner to Jerry's corner
And back to Avenue Road.

Run, run, *puff, puff,* round the bend I go,
I'm only eight and I'm the bait
Round the bend I go.

Run, run, *puff, puff,* over the road I go,
Can I make it? Probably not,
Over the road I go.

Run, run, *puff, puff,* to the finish line I go,
Will I make it? A little bit faster,
Drink, drink, break, break, win, win.

Beatrice Vaughan (9)
Charlton CE Primary School, Dover

The Lost Cat

Is it here? Is it there?
Is it coming for me?
I just cannot see,
Why it's coming for me.
I think it's over there,
I'm staring hard, but I cannot see
What is stalking me.
I build up my courage,
To go and see
What is stalking me.
Then I look and I see
A cat reading a book
Just like me.

Nicole Larke (9)
Charlton CE Primary School, Dover

Sports

Football, football is the best,
You don't need an under vest.

Tennis, tennis is so great,
Your match is at 4 o'clock, you can't be late.

Dance a lot, dance a lot,
You don't need to be Sir Lancelot.

Swimming, swimming is brilliant exercise,
You need to wear your goggles over your beady eyes.

Matthew Cragg (8)
Charlton CE Primary School, Dover

Families

Brother crying every night,
Sisters having a fight,
Mum doing the washing for us,
Dad saying she must.

Dog barking at me,
Dad climbing a tree,
Friend saying hooray,
Mum saying it's a good day.

Brother laying on his head,
Dad putting me to bed
House is quiet,
For the rest of the night.

Vikki Uden (9)
Charlton CE Primary School, Dover

Guinea Pig

I've got a guinea pig,
Sitting on a hutch,
She eats carrots,
But not that much.

Her nickname is Gizzy,
Because she gets dizzy,
People think she's silly,
But that's just Lily.

Isabel Lily Marples (8)
Charlton CE Primary School, Dover

Brothers

Brothers are annoying,
Brothers are cool,
Brothers are nice,
But mine is a fool.

Sean Knight (9)
Charlton CE Primary School, Dover

Slowly

Slowly the tide comes in,
Slowly the sand sticks in-between my toes,
Slowly the seagulls glide in the sky,
Slowly the birds sing a song,
Slowly a starfish rises from the sand.

Jasmine Alice Kember (8)
Charlton CE Primary School, Dover

Dog Emotions

A shih-tzu is a moany dog,
A German shepherd is a guard dog,
An Akita is a jumpy dog
And they all have their own emotions.

A border collie is a happy, jolly dog,
A bulldog is a chubby dog,
A Staffordshire bull terrier is a fierce dog
And they all have their own emotions.

A Chihuahua is very small,
A Great Dane is very tall,
A whippet is very thin
And they all have their own emotions.

Jake Smissen (9)
Charlton CE Primary School, Dover

Cat In The Window

Cat in the window,
What do you see?

Stars, moon, owls,
An owl gliding through the trees,
The bluebells shivering in the untimely snow,
The fluffy white clouds that are very low.

Trees, lovely and green,
Birds tweeting loudly,
Children screaming I've seen,
Red berries on the bushes,
Sparkly light blue sky.

Charlotte Brooke-Pearce (7)
Cleves School, Weybridge

Wings
(Based on 'If I Had Wings' by Pie Corbett)

If I had wings
I could touch the shining, sparkling stars,
That twinkle above us.

If I had wings
I could taste the cheesy moon.

If I had wings
I could see Big Ben from far away.

If I had wings
I could fly over
The beautiful, colourful rainbow.

Gaby Gleeson (8)
Cleves School, Weybridge

Cat In The Window

Cat in the window
What do you see?

Houses, cars, fireworks
The exploding colours above a tree.

The smoke going from the fireplace
Fluttering into the sky
The leaves crumbling like torn paper
And the air lifting them high.

Rain pitter-pattering on the icy ground
Snow swirling down
Frost brushing on the cold rooftops
The gleaming white snow covers the sleeping town.

Sophie Denham (8)
Cleves School, Weybridge

Wings
(Based on 'If I Had Wings' by Pie Corbett)

If I had wings
I would touch the Taj Mahal in India.

If I had wings
I would taste the freezing rain as cold as ice.

If I had wings
I would listen to the wonderful fireworks glittering in the night sky.

If I had wings
I would smell the smoke of hot dogs on the burning barbeque.

If I had wings
I would gaze at the clouds looking like they are moving.

If I had wings
I would dream of the hot sun and people going to the moon.

Sally Hoyle (7)
Cleves School, Weybridge

Cat In The Window

Cat in the window
What do you see?

Clouds, bluebells, fox
A fox sleeping under a tree
Fireworks booming in the night sky
Crash, crack, banging up high.

Rain dripping
Berry bushes waving
Enormous owls singing
A beautiful ladybird crawling
Dark night is arriving
A shining star is falling.

Robyn Edwards (7)
Cleves School, Weybridge

My Favourite Sport: Cricket

On match day,
I wake up at eight o'clock,
All ready and fit.
We drive to school,
Have some lessons
And the match will soon start.
I am in the changing rooms,
I can smell the sweat off everyone's body.
At the beginning,
The captains go to the middle of the pitch,
For the toss.

When batting,
I feel excited and nervous,
If I score lots of runs,
I feel happy.
I look where the fielders are
And I try to hit the ball into the gaps.
I can smell the match tea cooking,
From out in the middle.
The ropes shakes when I hit them,
With the cricket ball.
There is a bang when I hit the side screens.

When bowling,
I try to get a wicket,
I try to bowl the ball on the stumps every time.
When I get a wicket, I feel very happy.
I am a fast bowler
That bowls away swing,
It swings away from the batsman,
Making them edge it,
The wind helps it swing.

When fielding,
I try to catch everything
And some with stopping too.
I hear the birds singing
And the roaring of trains too.

I am happy with my team mates,
If they get a wicket,
I see all the wooden fences,
I also feel the breeze of the wind.

The game is over,
If we have won, I feel very pleased,
If we have lost, I feel disappointed.
I feel very tired afterwards,
Because I know I have tried my best.

Alexander Cook (9)
Edge Grove School, Aldenham Village

Edge Grove

Edge Grove is a place where you would like to be,
With all the teaching, fun and sporting activities.
All the children are different in every single way
And sometimes our mums ask us, 'What have you learnt today?'

The teachers have the knowledge to give us so much joy,
They give a lot of experience to lots of girls and boys.
With all the friends and all the work (we have quite a lot),
With all the lessons, Edge Grove is making young children
                                                go up to the top!

We are so lucky to go to such a great school,
That we should think of others and remember the rules.
Our school is a great place to be,
You can use your imagination and let your mind be free.

Thank you to all the staff of Edge Grove School,
You make learning so cool!

Oreoluwa Olubode (7)
Edge Grove School, Aldenham Village

Sports

Football is my favourite sport
I jump and bounce all day,
When it comes to football
I always have to play.

Rugby is rough and tough
Played only by the brave,
The ball is such a silly shape
It's a sport I really crave.

Cricket is a summer sport,
With eleven in your team,
There is batting, bowling and fielding -
Not to play would be really mean.

Hockey is a game with sticks
You use a putt or ball,
I like to play it on Astroturf
Because on ice, the putt is small.

Running is a sweaty sport
I am very good at it,
I like to run for miles and miles
Because it makes me fit.

Archery is a skilful sport
Bow and arrow must be used,
You have to hit the target
Otherwise you will lose.

Tennis is a game with rackets
The first shot is called a serve,
You run around from side to side -
Can you keep your nerve?

Swimming is a tiring sport
With lengths and strokes involved,
It's really not my favourite sport
Because the water is often cold!

Ned Holland-Hibbert (7)
Edge Grove School, Aldenham Village

I Wish I Were A Spaceman

I wish I were a spaceman,
I love to jump and shout
And when my mother calls me,
I say I'm going out.

I get into my rocket
And whizz up to the moon
I wave goodbye to mother
And say I'll be back soon.

I met a two-headed monster
He reminded me of my brother
He smiled at me with one head
And spat at me with the other.

Twice around the moon
I'll be home soon
Take care now, hold her steady,
'Howdy Mum, it's been such fun, is my dinner ready?'

James Nutt (7)
Edge Grove School, Aldenham Village

Swimming

The striking smell of chlorine hangs in the air,
The freezing water of the pool affects me immensely.
The sound of people shouting and calling me
And shouting, 'Jump Harvey, jump!' *Splash!*
I did a cannonball into the water.

Now I understand why they shouted 'jump Harvey, jump'
Because I now say it myself to my friends,
'Jump George, jump!'
The smell of the chlorine stills hangs in the air
And the pool has grown in warmth immensely
Yet when I swim I grow colder . . . colder . . . *colder!*

Harvey Presence (9)
Edge Grove School, Aldenham Village

I Wonder Why

I wonder why
My toys can't fly
But I can always
Make them cry
But still I can't
Make them fly.

So first I ask
My dad, but he
Says, 'Oh no, oh no,
I'm doing my show.'
But still I can't
Make them fly.

Then I go and ask
My mum, but she
Says, 'Oh no, oh no,
I'm doing my sums.'
But still I can't
Make them fly.

Then lastly,
I just ask my sister,
But she says, 'Oh no,
Oh no, I'm doing
My twister.'
But still I can't
Make them fly.

Then finally I think,
What to do.
I know!
I'll give them to you.

Rohit Biswas (7)
Edge Grove School, Aldenham Village

The Witch

A little green witch
With a teeny broomstick
With a small cottage house
And a cat
She has a wart on her nose
And some spiders in her hair
And some black, shiny lipstick on her lips
Her eyes are like a ball of fire
Her hair is like a black untidy knot
And I don't think you'll want to live with her!

Amy Edmeads (9)
Four Elms Primary School, Edenbridge

The Ice Tree

Frozen solid and stiff like an ivy tree
Once alive but now frosted
Into a frozen crisp tree.
Now the tree looks like
An ice-tree wizard.
The tree is looking
Like an ice tree.

Aaron Freeman (7) & Sam Moseley (8)
Four Elms Primary School, Edenbridge

Winter Wonderland

The frosty snow was an ice breath
The cold-covered trees
Were glistening in the sunlight
And the silky snow covered
The wrinkly, old tree.
The death-cold frost shivered the hedge
The stiffness of the hedge pricked up like the porcupines
People were snowed out of their lovely beds and homes.

Luke Burns (9) & Patrick Collier (8)
Four Elms Primary School, Edenbridge

Crystal Ice

When it's cold and wintry the white blanket of frost
sparkles like moonlight.
The frosty, white, crystal leaves and branches
send out a sprinkle of light like sunshine.
People breathe misty breath that settles on windows
and makes icy patterns on cars.
Young children slide on icy puddles
that sparkle under their feet.
Icicles hang from the houses that let out a warm glow
of winter light from their warm, cosy, curtained windows.
The freezing path to school is made up of icy crystal grass
that shimmers and shines the whole day long.
Birds sing winter songs with sparkling notes.
The misty blue sky has an endless line of wispy, light
frost grey clouds that drop
silvery, delicate, crystal snowflakes to the ground.
The swings in the park sparkle like twilight.

Sarah Partridge (9)
Four Elms Primary School, Edenbridge

A Day In The Water

I had a dream
And it came true
That I swam two lengths
Just like you.
I swam in the ocean
High and low
Until I reached the sky
I saw fish, fat and thin
Swimming with their colours loud and proud
I shimmered in the sun
I had a shining tail
Can you guess what I am?

Samantha Tilley (7)
Four Elms Primary School, Edenbridge

My Sister Said . . .

My sister said
Pets were allowed
In class 1
So . . . I went as a lion
But that was too scary.
I went as a sheep
But that was too hairy.
I went as a pig
But that was too pink.
I went as a skunk
But really did stink.
I went as a snake
But couldn't stay awake.
I went as a cat
But Mrs Winter didn't allow that.
So . . . I went as a giraffe
And we had a good laugh.

Mollie Longhurst (7)
Four Elms Primary School, Edenbridge

Rainbows

Rainbows have lots of different colours
Red, orange, yellow, green and blue
Indigo and violet too
They live up in the sky
Showing their lovely colours
When the sun shines
And the rain drips.

Emily Longhurst (6)
Four Elms Primary School, Edenbridge

A Flea

Oh, what fun, I am a flea
At present I am living in quiet Class 3

My perch is on a long, large stick, it wibbles and wobbles
And ink leaks from it

I love to slide on this gooey wet
I sometimes get stuck when the ink is set

I work myself loose and give a few jumps
Oh, a big square plank just gave me a bump

I've fallen in a tunnel, it's sharp at the sides
Oh, a big spike's coming, where can I hide?

I've jumped out of there and fallen on a square
Getting dizzy being moved here and there

Where can I go? I'll hide in this drawer
Oh no, more colours and books galore!

I've got to get out, there's no rest for this flea
I need to escape from noisy Class 3!

Isobel Money (7)
Four Elms Primary School, Edenbridge

History

It's just like any other subject
But just about different years
Everyone's learning lots of things
History is its name.

From Ancient Greeks to Romans
There are a dozen things to explore
And a lot more things to discover
The teacher's moaning and children are groaning
History is its name.

Zoe Priston (8)
Four Elms Primary School, Edenbridge

How The World Began

In the middle of nowhere . . .
Drips start making a salty sea,
Things with two fins sway,
There are big ones, little ones,
These are slimy fish.

Then the fish start to grow,
Tiny legs and then a tiny tail,
They are crazy and hop about,
These are mad amphibians.

But when the trees start to grow,
There is not any water,
The fish die but in their place,
Stand long chompers.
These are dangerous dinosaurs

It starts to get cold
And the dinosaurs die,
But now stand,
Fierce, strong mammals.

The mammals still prowl around,
But things with four legs,
They swing and sway,
These are active apes.

The apes start to grow hair,
Legs, hands and feet,
They play games and have fun,
These are playful humans
And this is how the world begun.

Hope Fuller (8)
Four Elms Primary School, Edenbridge

The Mouse In The House

There was a mouse that lived in a house
He was so rude; he ate all the food,

He ate all the jam, the cheese and the ham
He gnawed through the door, eating more and more

He never did stop, he even ate the mop!
Day and night, giving everyone a fright

Then along came a lady and her name was Cilla,
She brought a large bottle of industrial strength mouse killer

The cheeky mouse swallowed it and ran home in pain
And the poor little mouse was never seen again!

Milly Money (7)
Four Elms Primary School, Edenbridge

Spelling

I like spelling,
I do it all the time,
But when I don't do my homework,
It doesn't come out fine.

But when I try hard
And work really well,
My spelling comes back
And the marks are just really, really well.

Melody Bicknell (7)
Four Elms Primary School, Edenbridge

Riddle

I have seas with no water,
Coasts with no sand.
Towns with no people,
Mountains, no land.

I have rivers with no fish,
Air with no flies,
Gyms with no gymnasts,
The world with no skies.

Answer: a map.

Caitlin Kickham (9) & Michaela Haynes (8)
Four Elms Primary School, Edenbridge

Enchanted Forest

This forest is a place of dreams,
Where spirits roam around,
The magic of the ancients,
Lays sleeping, within the ground.
As the moon shines bright,
And the stars begin to wake,
Extraordinary plants,
Drink from the tiny lake.
The water is mystical,
So, shoots begin to grow,
And the glistening green grass,
Is a feast, for the waiting doe.

Andrew Gledhill-Carr (11)
Four Elms Primary School, Edenbridge

My Dog, Nala

Her eyes glisten a hazel brown full of love and grace,
As she runs along my side, everything's a race!
Her warm and boisterous smile fills me up inside,
Of all the peaceful feelings, most of all there's pride.
My dog's golden coat, as dark as a lion's mane,
She's always there to protect me in floods or hurricanes.
My dog, Nala!

Aston Bradshaw (11)
Four Elms Primary School, Edenbridge

The Angry Wave

The waves will crash on the water,
Blue cold will change to white warm.
The volcano controls the waves,
The wave will get angry.

David Whitford (9)
Kingsnorth CE Primary School, Ashford

The Crashing Waves

The waves crashing in the water
The top of the waves look like candyfloss
When the waves go round and round
It looks like a swirling vortex.

Dominic Osborne (9)
Kingsnorth CE Primary School, Ashford

The Little Raindrop

The sun on the sea was shining
Lots and lots of people were holding hands
A little water drop was rising
Children played in the sands.

Maisey Twomey (10)
Kingsnorth CE Primary School, Ashford

The Water Drops Of Wonderful Things

The sun on the sea was shining,
There were people in the sea,
As the little water drop was rising,
Catching things, like catching us three.

The lightning it was lashing,
People at home having tea,
While the fishermen fished in the sea,
Racing the ground, the rain was dashing.

The ocean was evaporating,
The sun blew in the morning sky,
Racing to the ground, the rain was dashing,
The clouds were rising high.

Richard Phillip Wilson (9)
Kingsnorth CE Primary School, Ashford

The Little Raindrop

The sun on the sea was shining,
But the sea didn't make a sound,
As the little raindrop was rising,
Then the raindrop formed a cloud.

As the howling wind was blowing,
Seagulls were making squeaking noises,
Then the grey clouds made thunder and lightning,
Then I heard some loud voices.

Soon I saw the clouds were raining
And everybody was running loudly,
The aggressive blue waves started bashing,
As the people walked by soundly.

Ashleigh Ann Wheal (9)
Kingsnorth CE Primary School, Ashford

The Sea

The sun was shining,
There were people swimming in the sea,
Things catching us three,
As the little water drop was rising.

The ocean was evaporating,
The sun ablaze in the morning sky,
Racing to the ground the rain was dashing,
The clouds were all rising.

The lightning in the sea was flashing,
While the fishermen were fishing in the sea,
Racing to the ground the rain was dashing,
The clouds were rising high.

Farid White (9)
Kingsnorth CE Primary School, Ashford

The Little Raindrop

The sun on the sea is shining,
The sky as blue as midnight,
As the little water drop is shining,
I gaze upon the lovely sight.

The boats in the sea are rowing,
As the mountains,
You can't miss the very loud clouds crashing,
The lightning flashes brilliantly.

The clouds in the sky are hitting,
Making lots of noise as they rush by,
The water is in a nice calm flowing,
Great paintings of the cool sky.

Emily Joy Harris (10)
Kingsnorth CE Primary School, Ashford

Fish

The lightning was lashing in the sky,
Racing to the ground, the rain was dashing,
Fishermen's relatives saying goodbye
And the waves were crashing.

The filthy raindrop fell to the sea weeping,
While fishermen were fishing at sea,
Meagre raindrops are always dreaming,
People at home having tea.

Some fishermen are lost at sea
And relatives are so sad and are sobbing,
Cods and halibuts in the sea are tossed,
The water buoys are bobbing.

Will Flockett (9)
Kingsnorth CE Primary School, Ashford

The Water Adventure

The sun on the sea was shining,
But the sea didn't make a sound,
As the little water drop was rising,
Then the water drop formed a cloud.

As the wind was moving,
The cloud was floating above,
But as the birds were singing,
The cloud was quiet as a dove.

Now that it's raining,
The water forms a river,
It leads to the sea which is splashing,
This makes it even bigger.

Natasha Francis (10)
Kingsnorth CE Primary School, Ashford

The Little Raindrop

The sun on the sea was shining,
While the birds were singing so sweetly,
As the little water drop was rising,
She was laying down so quietly.

Suddenly the wind was blowing
And the little cute water drop woke up by luck,
But then she saw the beautiful sighting
And fell right next to a duck.

The little raindrop was evaporating,
Saying goodbye to all her friendly friends,
She met some new friends when she was falling
And saw others on weekends.

Joanne Sheppard (9)
Kingsnorth CE Primary School, Ashford

The Water Drop

The sun on the sea was shining,
The sea started to get rough,
As the little water drop was rising,
The water was getting tough.

The sun on the sea was shining,
The dolphins were jumping through the waves,
As a little cool rain was falling,
The sharks were going through the caves.

William Ashdown (9)
Kingsnorth CE Primary School, Ashford

The Beach

The sun on the sea was shining,
As the seagulls were fishing for some krill,
The frightful heavy clouds started bashing,
As the sea and I stood still.

The sea was twirling and swirling,
The waves were crashing into the rocks,
Some people were still out at sea sailing,
I was playing near the docks.

The day was sunny, I went surfing,
The crabs were crawling around the sand,
Up in the sky, the seagulls were flying,
My friend saw a piece of land.

Orla McGlone (9)
Kingsnorth CE Primary School, Ashford

Flowing Of The Sea

The sun on the sea was shining,
There were people swimming in the sea,
As the little water drop was rising
And things were catching us three.

The fish in the sea were jumping,
Killer whales lurking for their supper,
The clever dolphins are always bumping,
Little whale with its mother.

The sun on the ocean was blazing,
The surfers were surfing through the sea,
There were lots and lots of people gazing,
People were going home for tea.

Molly McKeown (9)
Kingsnorth CE Primary School, Ashford

Travelling

The sun on the sea was very bold,
While the people on the beach were talking,
When the people on the beach were cold,
The baby was not crying.

The lightning on the sea was lashing,
While the fishermen were fishing in the sea,
Racing to the ground, the rain was dashing,
People at home having their tea.

The wind in the air was windy,
While the clouds in the sky were moving,
Then the bad wind got extremely speedy,
The people were all shaking.

Ben Harte (9)
Kingsnorth CE Primary School, Ashford

The Adventures Of A Raindrop

The waves were travelling through the docks,
Away the aggressive crab was floating,
The raindrop was sitting on the big rock,
But the crab was still floating.

When the fishermen were fishing,
The frightened fish were floating through the docks,
The rough ocean was swirling and twirling,
The crab sat on the rocks.

As the loud seagulls were squawking,
The thunderous clouds were bashing together,
As the tremendous big waves were rising,
The cycle goes on forever.

George Paul (10)
Kingsnorth CE Primary School, Ashford

The Seaside

The blue and green sea was warming,
The dolphins were jumping through the waves,
The warming, pebbly sea was rough, splashing,
Birds were calling from the caves.

The lightning on the sea was lashing,
While the fishermen were fishing at sea,
Racing to the ground, the rain was dashing,
People at home having tea.

The green and blue sea was calming,
The fishing boats were sailing to the docks,
The seaside had fish swimming and jumping,
The waves were smashing on the rocks.

Martin Nichols (10)
Kingsnorth CE Primary School, Ashford

Breaking Free

The sun was shining on the seas,
The raindrop was evaporating,
While the dolphins were like busy bees,
The fluffy clouds were moving.

The raindrop turned into a cloud,
The little cloud was twirling and whirling,
The little birds were very, very loud,
The really loud wind was howling.

It started to rain on a mountain,
The raindrop to the ground was falling,
The raindrop became part of a fountain,
Having fun splashing and crashing.

Kayleigh Winn (9)
Kingsnorth CE Primary School, Ashford

The Raindrop

The sun on the sea was shining
And the sun was making lots of clouds,
As the little water drop was falling,
Raindrops are having dreams.

The sun was coming up and beaming,
On the river and in the big blue sea,
The sun is looking at stuff melting,
In the South and North Poles.

The clouds in the sky are hitting
And the lightning was making lots of noise,
They were making lots and lots of lightning,
Which is very dangerous.

Jamie Nichols (10)
Kingsnorth CE Primary School, Ashford

Water Flows

The colourful waves are crashing,
While they crash against the dock,
The day has just begun, yet it's raining,
People inside have their doors locked.

The clouds are singing in a fine way,
As the boats bob up and down,
Everyone is happy today,
No one has yet a frown!

While people are on the beach,
Children dig in the sand,
While seagulls screech over the beach,
While listening to the seaside band.

Amber Court (9)
Kingsnorth CE Primary School, Ashford

The Raindrop

The very rough waves were crashing,
The dark, greeny-blue water went high,
Not knowing where the water was going,
The water looked up at the sky.

The sun on the sea was shining,
The dolphins were jumping through the waves,
Multicoloured fish were running and dashing,
People going through the caves.

The water was quietly crashing,
The water was coming up to a tide,
The big tidal wave was gently swirling
And the people were hiding.

Jack Sims (10), Callum Booth & Dan Bottachi (9)
Kingsnorth CE Primary School, Ashford

The Water Flows

The sun on the sea was shining,
The dolphins were jumping through the waves,
As the little water drop was rising,
The birds were calling from the caves.

The lightning was bashing and crashing,
The waves were smashing against the rocks,
The clouds were moving as the sky was twirling,
The waves were still crawling up the rocky cracks.

The surfers started surfing,
Having fun on the seaside,
The wonderful, glittery waves started moving,
There was a fair on the other side.

Eleanor Denniss (10)
Kingsnorth CE Primary School, Ashford

Haunted House

Creepy doctors pulling out teeth,
Skeletons jumping up and down,
Ghostly ghosts haunting the streets,
Massive spiders spinning cobwebs in the cracks,
Ferocious bats hanging from the wall,
Ugly beasts hunting for their food,
Screaming, howling, creepy, booming,
These are the noises of my haunted house.

Danny Theobald (10)
Larkrise Primary School, Chelmsford

Deck Of Cards

Hearts, diamonds, spades and clubs
Jacks, queens and kings
You can play away for a day
Thinking quick and being slick
Games are fun to play.
Learning, churning, flipping over
You can add and take away
Use the deck to play and play
Every single day.

Jordan Northrop (10)
Larkrise Primary School, Chelmsford

Speed

Speed
Getting scary, too fast
Losing control
Take a corner, slow down
Handling much better
Been overtaken, speed up
Trying to gain 1st position
Speed.

Ben Howard (11)
Larkrise Primary School, Chelmsford

Penguins

Slipping, sliding across the ice
The cold is setting in
Waddling through the cold Atlantic
Squawking for the fish
Sliding on their bellies
Not giving a care
Making holes in the ice
Into the icy, cold water
Going down
Down, down, down
Floating down
Gliding through the water.

Marnie Bevan (11)
Larkrise Primary School, Chelmsford

Poppies

People dying
Babies crying
One more poppy appears

Lying on the ground
Loads of bodies around
Two more poppies appear

Letters to wives
Their losing their lives
Three more poppies appear

Head pouring with blood
Lying in a pile of mud
Four more poppies appear.

Jessica Hubbard (10)
Larkrise Primary School, Chelmsford

Winnie The Pooh

There once was a bear
His name was Pooh
He loved to eat honey too.

He lived in a tree
Not far from the honey tree
So when he ran out
He didn't have far to go
To get some honey for his tummy.

Pooh had lots of different friends
Their names were Christopher Robin
Piglet, Rabbit, Tigger, Roo, Kanger, Owl and Eeyore.

Christopher Robin sometimes said,
'You silly old bear.'

So that's what Pooh had
And there is what Pooh did
He was just a funny little bear
With a very little mind.

Kimberley Brewster (11)
Larkrise Primary School, Chelmsford

Cars

Cars may be supersonic
Cars may be like a snail
Cars may be shiny
Like the colours of the rainbow.

Cars may be old and rusty
Cars may be crystal new
Cars may be anything
But they are always great.

Lewis Hilden (11)
Larkrise Primary School, Chelmsford

Monkeys

Swinging along through the trees
Bending their little knees
Helping to swing along
They begin to hum a song.

Long hairy bodies love to climb
Up, up, up, up to the vines
Then he falls and runs around
Treading on bugs that are on the ground.

Monkey, monkey, full of fun
Running around in the red-hot sun
Monkey, monkey, you're so hairy
But you are so cute, you can't be scary.

Swinging through the trees
Bending their little knees
Helping to swing along
They begin to hum a song.

Bryoni Dale (11)
Larkrise Primary School, Chelmsford

Tornado

Spinning, swirling,
Crashing, curving,
Round the tornado spins.

Banging, booming,
Roaring, soaring,
Whizzing round and round.

Run, run, all scream and shout
As it gets closer to them, just about.

But then the tornado turns out
Dies out
Now it has gone without a doubt
Yeah!

Ashleigh Sinden (10)
Larkrise Primary School, Chelmsford

Monster!

We are walking along a dark, dark street,
All we can hear is the sound of our feet,
We hear a noise and turn around,
But no one's there,
We ignore the sound.
I hear a *bang!*
I scream, I run,
No one's there,
But still we run and run.
Eventually we leave the street,
We stop, but we still hear feet.
I turn around,
Someone's there,
Coming closer, but we can't move,
I can see him now,
In all his glory,
His blood-red eyes, his razor teeth,
He's right up close,
Closer, closer,
We all shout out,
Monster!

Nathan Watkinson (11)
Larkrise Primary School, Chelmsford

The Sea

T wirling waves
H urling stones
E els are wriggling

S wirling seas
E ndless roaring
A lways crashing

Dripping, tipping along hurling stones.

Shaun Evans (10)
Larkrise Primary School, Chelmsford

Ninjas

Punching, kicking, flipping, tripping
Karate chopping, self defence
Let the battle commence
Swords clanging, crossbows firing
Death stars flying, Nunchuckers spinning
Daggers stabbing, punching, kicking, flipping, tripping
Karate chopping
Self defence, let the battle commence
Samurais slaughtering, axes slashing
Fighting to the death.

Harry Charlick (10)
Larkrise Primary School, Chelmsford

Shopping

From Chanel to Gucci,
Gucci to Chanel,
We're gonna hit the mall
For a new wardrobe.

I love my shoes,
I love my tops
D&G rocks!

Diamonds are my bling,
Gems are just not my thing,
I wear my D&G flipflops every day,
I wear my Gucci dress on a special day.

Christie Schott (10)
Larkrise Primary School, Chelmsford

Wouldn't It Be Funny?

Wouldn't it be funny,
If you didn't have a nose?
You couldn't smell your mummy,
If you didn't have a nose.
You couldn't smell the ocean,
Or the traffic, I suppose.
You couldn't wear your glasses,
If you didn't have a nose.

Wouldn't it be funny,
If you didn't have a mouth?
You couldn't talk to anyone,
Or even answer a question,
Or even tell your mummy,
That you broke two eggs.

Wouldn't it be funny,
If you had cheese as toes?
People would walk past and say,
'There goes smelly toes!'
Oh, oh, wouldn't that be funny!

Chahat Shah (11)
Monega Primary School, London

The Boogieman

B oogieing all the time in the night
O ut in the open, in the spotlight
O n the whole I can only say
G et dance lessons, OK
I t is a real pain to see him move
E specially when he is in his moody groove
M y gosh, he drives me mad
A rgh! He is just so, so bad
N othing will get worse than my dad, the *boogieman!*

Isabel Fanfan (11)
Monega Primary School, London

The Monkey And His Present

Down by the bay,
Where I go to stay,
I saw a monkey saying,
'Hip, hip, hooray,'
When his mother bought him a little toy,
'Thank you, Mother,
You're the best,
Better than all the rest,
But I really wished to have a vest,
Because it is freezing cold,
Out in the west.'

Junaid Mahmood (10)
Monega Primary School, London

Da Bogeyman!

Who's that bump in the night?
Who's always giving you scares?
Who is always at the door?
Who is always in your nightmares?

It's da bogeyman!

'Who's always making you scream?
Who's that little creep?
Who's always making you cry?
Who's always making you leap?

It's da bogeyman!
'I'm coming
        To
            Get
                You!'

Tasnima Khanom (11)
Monega Primary School, London

True Friends

A true friend is someone who
Will always be there for you
And stand by you no matter what,
Through the good times and the bad.

A true friend will never lie to you,
They will never let you down,
They will always remain loyal and truthful to you,
Someone you can rely on and trust.

A friend who will jump off a tree,
Because they believe and have faith in you,
That you will be there, waiting to catch them
And pull them back to safety.

A real friend is someone
Who you can share your worst moments with,
Because you know that they will support you
All the way through . . .

A *true* best friend is like a four-leaf clover,
Very hard to find, but lucky to have,
Precious and special.

Rima Akthar (11)
Monega Primary School, London

Animals

Animals in the jungle,
Animals in the sea,
Animals in the savannah,
Animals in the rainforest,
All of them with different,
Shapes and sizes,
We have fat animals,
Thin animals,
We have animals with big eyes,
Animals with small eyes,
What wonderful creatures they are!

Etse Umole (9)
Monega Primary School, London

Me!

Asian, Indian, Muslim, me,
British, western, English, me.

We eat different foods,
To suit our different moods,
Samosas, curry, chapattis,
Pizza, burgers, Smarties.

From top to toe will I dress
And never try to look a mess,
Muslim; religious shalwarkamies,
English, dresses, tops and jeans.

I try to be nice and fun,
Just like the bright, bright sun,
Talkative, hyper, warm and kind,
Been called weird, but I don't mind.

With my friends,
I try to make amends,
My friends mean a lot,
Like Pauline means to Dot.

I like who I am
And wouldn't change,
I'm not better than the rest
And I didn't say I was the best!

Ayesha Vali (11)
Monega Primary School, London

New Year's Day

New Year's here
Everyone's happy
To start a new year
That brings them joy

While everyone's having fun
Mums are busy in the kitchen
Making sweet dishes that are tasty

When everyone's full, they stop
And make resolutions
Which are crazy.

Iqra Ali (10)
Monega Primary School, London

Life

Days come and go,
Time passes by,
Tomorrow is another day
And it can't be denied.

You've got a life,
To do whatever you want,
Don't waste it,
Have a brilliant time.

There's a whole wide world,
Waiting for you,
I really need to go,
Because I've got to get to school.

Nalisha Arya (9)
Monega Primary School, London

Stormy Days

Today was a stormy day,
Well, in a different way.
It was dark and really frightful,
No one thought this was delightful.
Everyone was scared, ran to their house,
Everyone did, even a mouse.
It was a scary day, everyone cried,
I'm extremely surprised that nobody died.
Today was a really long day,
Well, in a different way.
You thought the day would have had an end,
Well, the next day had a new trend.
The day is brilliantly bright
And definitely not dark, but really light.
The sudden change is extremely good,
Nobody else thought the day would.

Dylan Dhinsa (9)
Monega Primary School, London

My Mother!

Here comes my mother,
With her brand new mop,
Splish over here,
Splish over there,
Cleaning, scrubbing everywhere,
Dusting all the cobwebs,
Beating all the mats,
Arranging all the furniture,
Hanging all the hats,
'Mother dear, what are you doing?'
She says, 'Son, don't you know your father's coming!'

Sumayyah Shabbir (10)
Monega Primary School, London

Friendship

Friendship is precious,
Keep it,
Protect it,
You will need it,
Don't throw it away,
Don't break it,
Don't neglect it,
Keep it somewhere -
In your heart,
If you want to -
But keep it,
For friendship has no boundaries,
As that of the world,
It is the colour of the rainbow
And it has the beauty of a dream.

Nazima Naznin (10)
Monega Primary School, London

Spooky Night

As I settle down to sleep,
I hear a rustling sound outside,
I look out, but there's nothing to be found,
In the sky, I see something fly,
Round and round it goes,
Flashing lights blind my eye,
A cold shiver runs down my spine,
I shiver and I shake,
As it disappears into the misty sky,
I stay awake, wondering, wondering
What it might be . . .

Jasmin Begum (11)
Monega Primary School, London

Nothing Else Left To Treasure

God has given us a speck of hope,
But we have tangled it into a rope,
Nothing else left to treasure.

God has given us those lovely smiles,
To open up those statement files,
Nothing else left to treasure.

God has given us a wonderful family,
That always has the biggest category,
Nothing else left to treasure.

God has given us the best gift in the world
And always remember, it is your *life,*
God has given us a lot to treasure.

Roshni Arya (11)
Monega Primary School, London

But Why!

I asked my teacher at school today,
Why chocolate is so sweet,
She answered back in a simple way,
'Would you rather it taste of feet!'

I asked a friend on the way home today,
Why cheese is so very smelly,
She answered me so very quickly,
'Well the smell's to alarm your belly!'

I asked my parents at home today,
Why fizzy drink is so fizzy,
They answered back in a rush,
'We don't know! Now go away, we're busy!'

I asked myself in the mirror today,
Why I ask people everything,
My reflection just stared back at me,
'Fine, don't say anything!'

Zakiyah Begum (11)
Monega Primary School, London

Love

It looks like a beautiful, pink, fluffy cushion laying on your bed,
It sounds like an angel fluttering its wings, up high in the sky,
It feels like a newly born chick with lots of fluffy feathers,
It tastes like chocolate melting on your tongue,
It smells like the scent when you walk into a garden full of roses,
It lives deep inside your heart and flies out when you're happy.

Chloe Vissers (10)
Newlands Primary School, Ramsgate

Love

Love is blue
It feels like a massive fluffy ball wrapped around your body
It smells like a freshly sprayed lady's perfume, which smells
                                                        like a rose
It tastes like pizza piled high with your favourite topping
It looks like a blowing daffodil on a humid spring day
It sounds like a blue-breasted kingfisher chirping on top of
                                                        a willow tree
It lives in every heart.

Jonathan Moore (10)
Newlands Primary School, Ramsgate

Love

Love is a highly cheering sensation
It gives off a light each day
Love shimmers and glimmers, love dances and prances
It's such a delight to give away
Love smells like your favourite bar of chocolate
Given to you on Valentine's Day
Love sounds like a magic white rabbit
Rustling around on an autumn day!

Jayde Storey (10)
Newlands Primary School, Ramsgate

Love

It feels like the passion of your heart
It sounds like roses being picked from a glistening flowerbed
In the morning frost
It tastes like the finest Belgian chocolate made on Earth
It looks like a candlelit restaurant full of loving eyes
It lives in the centre of your heart.

Sophie Allen (10)
Newlands Primary School, Ramsgate

Love

It sounds like the biggest pounding heart
It looks like a mouth-watering Turkish delight
It tastes like a cake smothered in chocolate
It feels like you're in an extraordinary world of your own
It lives in you, desperate to come out.

Ellie Simpson (11)
Newlands Primary School, Ramsgate

Love

It feels like a plump, soft, fluffy pillow,
It looks like the brightest red rose ever seen,
It sounds like the whistling of a bird as it flutters away,
It tastes like luscious melted chocolate
Being poured slowly into your mouth,
It lives in the light, beaming, glittering eyes
Of an eye-catching human being.

Samuel Clark (11)
Newlands Primary School, Ramsgate

Love

It smells like a powerful perfume,
Mixed with freshly picked flowers.
It tastes like golden honey,
Slowly trickling down your throat.
It sounds like a heartbeat,
Thudding against a layer of skin.
It feels like a silky cushion,
Warm and soft to the touch.
It looks like a golden rainbow,
Leading the way to happiness.
It lives in the heart of each of us,
Waiting for you to see the one.

Zak Cohen (10)
Newlands Primary School, Ramsgate

Love

Love looks like a gigantic part of Heaven
Bobbing up and down in the dazzling starlight
Love feels like a soothing, relaxing bath;
Massaging you all over
Love tastes like luscious chocolate
Running down your throat
Love smells like a million summer-scented roses
All in a row
Love sounds like a gigantic heartbeat
Fluttering up to happiness
Love lives in me and everyone
Love is everywhere.

Jack Warner (11)
Newlands Primary School, Ramsgate

Love

It looks like a vast heart-shaped cloud
Shining down on you from the blue skies
It sounds like a bird serenading his future
It feels like someone being there for you
And never letting go
It tastes like your favourite food
That you never want to stop eating
It lives down under your skin
And always wants to come out to find your perfect match.

Sean Fairhurst (11)
Newlands Primary School, Ramsgate

Love

Love is pink
It feels like your soul is full of desire
It sounds like the birds chirping on a blazing hot summer's day
It tastes of golden honey gradually trickling into your mouth
It lives in romantic hearts everywhere.

Jarrett Francis (11)
Newlands Primary School, Ramsgate

Love

Love is a beautiful sherbet pink
It looks like your true love standing on the doorstep
It smells like roses growing in my garden at springtime
It tastes like the most delightful chocolate cake
With juicy strawberries on top
It sounds like a newborn baby letting out its first cry
It feels like a huge fluffy pillow under my glistening cheek
It lives deep down . . . in the centre of our hearts.

Anastasia Batten (10)
Newlands Primary School, Ramsgate

Love

It looks like a fairy fluttering her gorgeous but delicate wings
It sounds like beautiful red roses falling gracefully from Cupid's sky
It smells like an oozing chocolate river
It tastes like a strawberry dipped into a deep pot
Of white glittering sugar
It feels like a newborn baby snuggling into your chest
It lives with me and you in our hearts forever.

Sian Hayes (11)
Newlands Primary School, Ramsgate

Love

It feels like a big ball of velvet.
It smells like roses on a summer's day.
It looks like a robin elegantly showing its red breast on a winter's day.
It sounds like a church choir singing gracefully.
It tastes like a luscious cup of tea.
It lives in everyone and it can never be stopped.

Limar Atiera (10)
Newlands Primary School, Ramsgate

Love

Love has the smell of fresh roses
Seeping through the small crack in your window
Love tastes like a delicious chocolate melting in your mouth
Love sounds like a harp being plucked by an angel
Love looks like a pure white dove perched on a blooming tree
Love lives deep in everyone's heart.

Megan Brown (11)
Newlands Primary School, Ramsgate

Love

Love tastes like the sweet substance in chocolate
It sounds like the whistling song that summer birds make
On a scorching day
It smells like searing honey trickling out of a golden bottle
It feels like the relaxing comfort that spreads around
Your body while laying in bed
It looks like tall swaying trees in the chilling breeze
It lives in the middle of your heart waiting to leap out!

Conor Hope (11)
Newlands Primary School, Ramsgate

Love

Love smells like my favourite dinner being cooked
And the smell drifting up to my room
It tastes like a warm, crispy potato being placed upon my tongue
Love feels like my big, huge, fluffy, extra-soft cushion
Tickling my face
It sounds like robins chirping beautifully
On a nice, hot summer's morning
It lives in warm, loving hearts and it should . . . forever.

Hanna Bowley (10)
Newlands Primary School, Ramsgate

Love Is Like . . .

Love is like my mum
Who makes me feel so nice
She gives me cuddles
When I think of my grandad
It makes me warm inside
Love is red.

Gabrielle Challis (8)
Newlands Primary School, Ramsgate

Love

It looks like roses being dropped from the sky
Onto a beautiful clear blue lake
It feels like the warm summer's air blowing your hair
Back into the glistening blue sea
It tastes like a chocolate bar bursting into your mouth
Like a volcano erupting
It sounds like a newborn baby chick easing itself out of its shell
And chirping for its mum
It smells like a new bottle of perfume
Made from teardrops and affection
It lives deep, deep inside your heart
Surrounded by care and kindness for all eternity.

Siâna Smith (11)
Newlands Primary School, Ramsgate

Love Is Like . . .

The birds chirping in my ear
Love is orange like the morning clouds
Love is like the cosiest eiderdown
Love is like the tastiest chocolate
Love is so romantic, I hardly know I'm alive.

Rachel Adkins (8)
Newlands Primary School, Ramsgate

Love Is Like . . .

Love smells like chocolate and flowers
Love looks like blossom, nice and pink
Love feels romantic and happy
A fairy with its wings
Love tastes like the air in the sky
Love is pink and red.

Katherine Stirrups (7)
Newlands Primary School, Ramsgate

Love Is Like . . .

Love is love
Love makes me happy
Smell the roses
Smell the scent
Love makes me happy
Love is deep
Love is sweet
Love makes me really happy
Love makes love.

Kye Boughton (8)
Newlands Primary School, Ramsgate

Love Is Like . . .

Love is like my mum
Love is like my dad
Love is like my pets
Love is like my aunties
Love is like my cousins
Love is like my nannies.

Olivia Turner (7)
Newlands Primary School, Ramsgate

Love Is Like . . .

I love my mum today
Roses to make her happy
I love my mum.

Kieran Horsley (8)
Newlands Primary School, Ramsgate

Love Is Like . . .

Love makes me happy
Love makes me warm
It's so romantic
It makes me feel cosy
It smells like blossom on the blossom tree
Love is all around the world
So spread it all across the Earth.

Darcey Bennett (8)
Newlands Primary School, Ramsgate

Love Is Like . . .

Love is colourful
Love is happy
Love smells like roses
Love looks like rainbows and blossoms
Love sounds like chirping
Love tastes like cherries and chocolate
Love is romantic.

Christian Pressagh (8)
Newlands Primary School, Ramsgate

Love Is Like . . .

Love is like something pink
Like blossom on the trees
It sounds like musical wings
It makes me feel so romantic
I cannot hear my ears in the
Love of pink.

Vickie Vizer (8)
Newlands Primary School, Ramsgate

Love Is Like . . .

Red birds and swaying trees
Minted flowers and bumblebees
Orange chocolates
Tastes so sweet
Some of these
Are our treats.

Jack Hanes-Callis (8)
Newlands Primary School, Ramsgate

Love Is Like . . .

Love is nice
Love is calm
Love is beautiful
Love is something wonderful
Love can be something very good
For people to be happy.

Harley Jones (7)
Newlands Primary School, Ramsgate

Love Is Like . . .

Love is like the smell of sweet roses
Love is like the sound of birds chirping in the sky
Love is like the colours of the rainbow
Love is like the blossom coming off the trees
Love is like a person watching a romantic film
That is what I think love is like.

Tilly Shakeshaft (8)
Newlands Primary School, Ramsgate

Love Is Like . . .

Love makes me feel like I am hugging my mum
Love smells like roses
Love looks like blossom
Love tastes like a chocolate bar
As a treat to eat.

Jack Burnap (7)
Newlands Primary School, Ramsgate

My Donkey

My donkey has fur as soft as silk,
As brown as the brownest chocolate,
Her eyes are as round as the sun in the sky,
Her ears are as pointed as a pencil.

Marguerite's nature's as sweet as sugar,
The spot on her nose is as white as milk,
Her temptation for carrots is as big as a rabbit,
Her heart is as big as the Earth.

She's as cheeky as a monkey,
But as loyal as a saint,
She's as naughty as a devil,
But as good as gold.

Marguerite is like my sun and moon,
As dark as a storm cloud,
Yet as light as a summer's day,
She is like my world.

Philippa Helen Rooney (11)
Oakfield School, Pyrford

Passion

Passion can be anything . . .
Football or baseball,
R 'n' B or slow jam,
Sweets or chocolate.

Lawyer or celeb,
Scientists or agent,
Police officer or singer.

Love or hate,
Good or bad,
Sunny or rainy.

Chinazo Orji (9)
Our Lady of Lourdes RC Primary School, London

Winter Wonderland

The silvery-white moon sparkles,
Like a crescent diamond in the sky.

Snow that covers the rooftops,
Is like a bitter blanket of down.

Snowmen sit in the blank garden,
Like frozen models in position.

Sharp, icy winds pinch your rosy-red cheeks,
Like a knife ripping at a scarlet, frozen apple.

There's something in the air tonight,
It's like a mystical magic all around us.

Winter is a wonderful time,
Wonderful, but cold.

Anna Midgley (10)
Radwinter CE Primary School, Saffron Walden

A Game Of Rugby

Fly-half punts,
Hooker jumps.

Forwards ruck,
Ball stuck.

Ball comes out,
Captain shout.

Scrum-half throws,
Centre on his toes.

Centre switches,
As quick as he flinches.

Full-back sprints,
It's tense.

Full-back scores,
Crowd applause.

They win,
Crowd sing.

They win the game,
Full of fame.

Ivan Karsten (11)
Radwinter CE Primary School, Saffron Walden

Tumble Dryer

It swishes round and round,
It is a heated whirlwind,
It vibrates on the floor
And sends the carpet rippling,
It is a cheetah running along speedily,
The red light beams like owls' eyes,
When it finally stops,
The lid is a hippo eating.

Alice Moore (11)
Radwinter CE Primary School, Saffron Walden

My Animal Poem

My white, fluffy, bush of a tail
Glitters in the sun
My home, the burrow
Dug in the finest grounds of the earth.

My ears, so long and they flop down
Until I hear something
They shoot up, strong and pointy
Collecting all the noise I can gather.

I spot my enemies, by getting on my back legs
Standing tall and proud
When I see them
As fast as lightning.

I hop back, leaving a rabbit-shaped
Pile of dust in my path
I dive into my burrow
To protect myself.

Max Clay (11)
Radwinter CE Primary School, Saffron Walden

A Horse

The tiny bay pony has a silky coat,
Like velvet.

Trots around the arena
As bouncy as a boat bobbing up and down.

Nuzzles me when he wants a treat.

Tails swishes swiftly,
As it's chasing flies.

The foal lies in the grass,
Like a medium grey rock.

The love between my pony and me
Is stronger than iron.

Victoria Vicary (10)
Radwinter CE Primary School, Saffron Walden

Bored Mole

I stay down in my hole,
Nothing to do, I'm just a mole.

It's been a boring winter down here,
Every night I shed a tear.

All I do is wriggle around,
I can't see, but I hear sound.

A little worm under my nose,
I have claws, but no toes.

I grab the worm with my mouth,
My tail is north, but my nose is south.

The undergrowth falls on my head,
The worm is as thin as a thread.

I gobble and chew,
I wait by a hole with my friend, Shrew.

So you see,
My life isn't just hey, diddle, dee.

It's all work, no play,
Always catching my prey.

I stay down in my hole,
Nothing to do, I'm just a mole.

Thea Rudder Logan (10)
Radwinter CE Primary School, Saffron Walden

Football Match - Kennings

Goal-shooter
Best-booter
Ball-kicker
Glory-nicker
Left-backer
Huge-hacker
Success.

Rhys Basham (11)
Radwinter CE Primary School, Saffron Walden

My Family

My mum is a beautiful, pink flamingo, dancing around the house
Her good looks attract men all over the globe
She is generous to everyone that she meets
She is a caring love heart, darting around the house
She is a funny laugh, breezing gently through the land
I love my mum.

My dad is a loud, snoring lion, snoring all night long
He is generous to every one of my friends
He is a Peter Pan that never grew up
He is the god of love
He is a good-looking 36-year-old
His head is a shiny patch of armour
He is the funniest man on Earth
I love my dad.

Charlie is a cheeky monkey, swinging around the house
He is a cute, little rabbit, always watching TV
He is a caring god, all around me
He is a mini version of me
He is an annoying feather, tickling you all the time
He is a helpful robot, always clearing up after you
He is the best brother in the world
I love my brother.

Jack Mitchison (10)
Radwinter CE Primary School, Saffron Walden

Pig - Kennings

Fat-trotter
Mood-hotter
Finger-biter
Lovely-fighter
Pigsty-mucker
Mud-smudger
Poo-rubber
Pig-flubber.

Eve Hillier-Clarke (11)
Radwinter CE Primary School, Saffron Walden

A Fistful Of Pacifists

A squawk of singers,
A skinhead of hairs,
A flight of fish,
A barrel of bears.

A church of hatred,
A ceiling of floors,
An atom of elephants,
A wall of doors.

A thimbleful of giants,
A war of nuns,
A shout of silence,
A kiss of guns.

A pocketful of earthquakes,
A stray of bees,
A stumble of ballet dancers,
An elbow of knees.

A rustle of rhinoceros,
A circle of squares,
A fistful of pacifists,
A trio of pairs.

Sam Larlham (10)
Radwinter CE Primary School, Saffron Walden

A Fistful Of Pacifists

A pond of ducks
An arrow of geese
A bundle of whales
A heart of guns
A yodel of singers
A stray of bees
A swam of fish
A war of nuns
A crowd of soldiers
A waddle of snakes.

Terry Duck (11)
Radwinter CE Primary School, Saffron Walden

Dragon!

His scales are green,
Like a lizard's.
His blood is cold,
Like a snake's.
His wings are wide and spread like an eagle's
His breath could evaporate,
A lake.

His roar is as loud,
As a race car's engine.
His speed is as fast
As a cheetah.
With claws as sharp,
As a bison's horns
And teeth make him
One vicious eater.
A flying giant,
A king of the sea,
Sometimes a walker,
Like you and like me.
Behold a dragon!

Dominic Byrne (11)
Radwinter CE Primary School, Saffron Walden

The Tiger

He is as stripy as a zebra,
As fast as a dart,
Thrown at a dartboard,
Tail as long as a metre ruler,
Teeth as sharp as a razor,
His ears are as fluffy as a wild cat.

Aidan Clarke (11)
Radwinter CE Primary School, Saffron Walden

The First Winter

The alfresco air greets me once again,
Like the new sun meeting morning darkness.

I see the dormant hedgehog,
Like an obsolete volcano, now forgotten.

A sudden chill marks the first winter morning,
Like a sign, an early warning.

The beautiful ruby and amber skies,
Like a scarlet sheet billowing before my eyes.

Winter's treasures are hidden away,
Like secrets untold, no one will see.

A blooming snowdrop marks the first winter morning,
Like a sign, an early warning.

The dew on the glossed grass flicks onto my face,
Like momentary showers on a warm summer's day.

Winter is creeping behind me,
Like a ghost of what you dread most.

A bare tree marks the first winter morning,
Like a sign, an early warning.

Touch the leaves, coated in delicate frost,
Like a jewel-encrusted crown.

Icy cold water drops on my shoulder,
Like a sign, an early warning.

When the icy water drops, it's clear,
It's come, the first winter's here.

Florrie Priest (11)
Radwinter CE Primary School, Saffron Walden

The Dog - Kennings

Rabbit-hunter
Biscuit-cruncher

Teeth-sharper
Loud-barker

Human-licker
Tail-flicker

Meat-eater
Feet-heater

Cat-hater
Chase-later.

Michael Coe (11)
Radwinter CE Primary School, Saffron Walden

Harriet Hedgehog

Harriet Hedgehog bold and smart,
Harriet Hedgehog has a big heart,

Harriet Hedgehog has brown spikes,
Harriet Hedgehog goes on hikes,

Harriet Hedgehog likes to play,
Even if it's a rainy day!

Harriet Hedgehog curls in a ball,
Harriet Hedgehog is so small.

This evening I looked and had a peep,
Harriet Hedgehog was fast asleep.

Harriet Wood (8)
Sandcross School, Reigate

The Stream Walk

Tizzy, tizzy, tizzy!
I'm sliding down the bank.
Down on my bottom, then suddenly
Splash!
In the water it's cold and muddy
Wading through the brown depths
It's up to my hips.
Now we're at the deep part
I'm going down further!
We're climbing over the log
I'm sliding forward
Splish, splash, splosh, picking myself up.
Moving on steadily
I'm caught upon a twig
Falling down, with a splash!
Uh oh!
Crocodiles about!
We have to be careful
Or . . .
Snap! Snap! Snap!
Now we're off the end
Up the muddy bank
S-l-o-w-l-y s-l-i-d-i-n-g d-o-w-n . . .
No!
I'll try again
At last, I'm out!
But covered in mud,
Now a walk back to the chalet
For a warm, wet shower!

Emma Elson (10)
Sandcross School, Reigate

Me And My Pinball Machine

I'm off to play pinball,
Ah, here I am,
Isla come on,
My turn now,
What Isla?
It-is-my-turn!
'No, mine! She cries,
OK, I say, irritated,
She pushes me,
I push her back,
She pushes me harder,
I push her harder,
She shoves me even harder
And . . . *ka-splat!* My back hits the pinball machine!
I'm in agony!
'Isla,' I say,
'Yep,' she answers,
'That hurt!' I reply,
I agree,
Are you OK pinball machine?
What about me?
What about you?
Nails hurt!
Megan, they would,
If you fell on them
Isla!

Megan Smith (10)
Sandcross School, Reigate

London Bombing

The train was packed with people, all queuing to ride,
To their normal offices, on a normal morning in July.

I was one of them, waiting quietly for a train,
That would take me into the heart of the ants' nest,
That is London.

I sat in a seat, I saw the bag,
I could have stopped it,
But I thought nothing of it.

A few minutes later, *bang!*
I was on the floor, screaming.

Everything was black, dark and smoky,
Someone grabbed my arm, pulled me out of the window
And into the station.

Lights clicked on, all around were firemen,
We ran out onto the street,
We heard a *crash!*
The train had collapsed.

I turned round, but the man held me back,
I found myself in an ambulance,
I found I had lost my hand, my whole hand,
I realised I was in agony.

Here I sit, a year later, telling you this story,
Just remember, just stop and remember,
That nothing, I repeat, nothing,
Can kill the human spirit,
Can kill the bravery,
Can kill the soul,
If we all unite, we can stop this terror,
Nothing can stop us, *nothing!*

Ellie Christie (10)
Sandcross School, Reigate

Spotlight

Well,
I'm here now,
I can't go back,
I'm going to do it,
I've got to do it,
I can't let the troop down,
Not now.
All 17 of us,
Are going to dance together,
We've come all this way,
I can't let my friends down,
Not now.

We're in our dressing room,
The group next door,
Are Irish!
I can't let *our* group down,
Not now.
Our principal - Ellie,
Shows us to the stage,
It's terrifyingly *huge!*
But I can't let the theatre down,
Not now.

We watch the other troops,
They're so professional,
It's us next,
Wish,
Me,
Luck!

Gemma Cathie (9)
Sandcross School, Reigate

My New Trousers Are Doing A Runner!

At Gaveston Hall
Walking back
    To our
        Chalets
After some nice cooked marshmallows,
                My
              Legs
            Are
            Starting
        To
        Get
      Really
    Cold,
Now, for some weird reason, all
The boys in chalet two, are staring at me,
With
    Their
      Jaws
        Dropped!
And their eyes just about to pop out!
              And
            Now I
          Think
        That
      New
      Perfume
    Works.
Disaster has struck!
Alex just pointed out that my trousers
Have fallen down!

Mark Reynolds (9)
Sandcross School, Reigate

Soap, Squeeze, Splat!

Mum's just told me
To clean my teeth,
It's so boring!
Why do I have to?
It's always the same,
Just toothbrush, toothpaste . . .
Hey! Sudden idea!
Where's the soap?
Aha!
Now, add a bit of water,
One little squeeze . . .
Wh-e-e-e!
There goes the soap!
Look at it fly!
Oh no!
It's Mum!
Nooooo!
Splat!
On Mum's head
Oh dear
Time to go!

Alex Chowne (9)
Sandcross School, Reigate

Monkeys

Swinging on the trees
All hands and knees
For they just love to play!

Basking in the sun
Having lots of fun
For they just love to play!

Even in the rain
They never complain
For they just love to play!

Especially when it's hot
They still run a lot
For they just love to play!

And when they're ill
They simply take their pill
For they just love to play!

Monkeys in the zoo.

Clodagh Wells (8)
Sandcross School, Reigate

Frost Forest

In a dark, frost-bitten wood
Shone a huge ball of fire.

Trees shook off their snow,
Stretched in the blazing sun.

As the snow fell again
It did battle with the scorching rays.

Small animals peered from
The cracks in their old decaying trunks.

The trees looked on,
Emotionless, rigid.

Too busy to mind another frost to fire battle.

Jonathan Day (9)
Sandcross School, Reigate

There's A Spider In The Shower!

Me, Gemma and Emily,
Are in the shower,
At Gaveston Hall,
There's a *scream!*
Gemma comes
Running from the opposite
Shower,
'There's a spider in the shower!
Get it out!
Get it out!'
Me and Emily,
Are trying not to laugh,
Gemma shakes,
'What's so funny?
I don't like spiders!'
We creep round
To the next shower,
There's this tiny, little thing!
I'm sitting on the bottom bunk,
Of the triple bunk-bed,
At Gaveston Hall,
There's a squeal,
'The spider's back!'
That night, Emma's asleep,
After we convince her,
The spider's gone,
There's a yelp,
The spider's back!
Next day we hear a squeal,
The curse of the dreaded spider has returned!

Megan Bailey (10)
Sandcross School, Reigate

Fairy Tales

One glass slipper,
One trip to the ball,
One magic mirror,
One first dance in the hall.

One mean, ugly beast,
One gingerbread house,
One long, tall beanstalk,
One man into mouse.

One girl with long hair,
One lump in the bed,
One mean old wolf,
One palace ahead.

One book closed shut,
One lamp turned low,
One baby to sleep,
Time for Mummy to go!

Eleanor Riches (8)
Sandcross School, Reigate

Apple

A pples are great
P acked together in a
P lastic bag
L ike them all
E ven if they're sour.

Abbie Taylor (9)
Scargill Junior School, Rainham

The Chilling Heart Of Darkness

Darkness is jet-black like the sky
When the clock strikes midnight.

It sounds like a steady pounding
Through my ears.

Darkness has a bitter, sharp taste
Like an orange, which is definitely not ripe!

Mist, drifting through a graveyard
Chills right to the bone - smells dreadful!

It looks like the heart of a monster
Full of evil, beating its last.

Darkness feels like nothing
Empty, floating nowhere.

It reminds me of a ghost
Searching for its loved one, in the cold, bleak nights.

Claire Penny (10)
Sibertswold CE Primary School, Dover

Wonderland

I wonder why the sky is blue?
Do you?
Yes, well, I'll give you a clue . . .
Because apples are red,
Dirt is brown,
Bananas are yellow,
Grass is green,
So the sky had to be blue,
Get it now?
I do!

Annabel Reville (11)
Sibertswold CE Primary School, Dover

Silence

S ilence is a silvery-grey mist that hangs
   over villages and towns
I it is as quiet as a mouse that is treading over a thick carpet
   wearing velvet slippers
L ying in wait for the loudness
   to come
E verywhere
   it treads
N either dead nor alive
   just there
C rying over the loudness
   so it is drowned out
E ven the loudest of sounds
   can't go on forever.
   Silence always follows.

Sarah Penny (10)
Sibertswold CE Primary School, Dover

Happiness

Happiness is the colour of all light colours
Happiness sounds like people laughing out loud
Happiness tastes like a mouth-watering pineapple
Happiness smells like a field of lavender
Happiness looks like lots of big smiley faces
Happiness feels like meeting your friend after a holiday
Happiness reminds me of my family.

Jacob Roberts (10)
Sibertswold CE Primary School, Dover

The Midnight Darkness

Darkness is the colour of black, like a candle that has been blown
                                                                    out of sight
It sounds like a drum, banging in my ear
It tastes like curry, sizzling in my mouth
It smells like hot, spicy sauce, wafting up my nose
It looks like black dots on a dartboard that are coming closer
                                                                    and closer
It feels like a hot volcano that is just erupting in the air
It reminds me of a lost boy trying to find his way . . .

Shannah Hall (11)
Sibertswold CE Primary School, Dover

Rainbows

Rainbows are a whole world of happiness!
Rainbows are a load of different colours!
When you stand under it, there's a shining light above,
When the rain comes and the sun's out too,
There's lots of colour for you and me!
There comes a rain cloud, so sad to see!
Here comes the rain, goodbye Rainbow,
Hope to see you tomorrow!

Laura Palmer (11)
Sibertswold CE Primary School, Dover

Storms!

Storm, storm, gale to gale, storm, storm
Going at 90 miles per hour
Rioting through the air!
Storm, storm, hurricane to hurricane, storm, storm
Ripping up everything
Power cuts scare all there!
Storm, storm, thunder to thunder, storm, storm
Causing fires everywhere!
Almost killing wildlife!
Storm, storm, tornado to tornado, storm, storm
Destroys everything
Causing havoc everywhere!
Storm, storm, tsunami to tsunami, storm, storm
Flooding everything
Killing thousands!

Oh look! A rainbow!

Brandon Forrest (10)
Sibertswold CE Primary School, Dover

The Play-Park

Mums talk about the daily news
The sandpit is occupied by the under-twos

Toddlers squabble over toys
Young girls play kiss chase with the boys

Teenagers chat about the latest soaps
They all discuss their lifetime hopes

Babies scream, ready for lunch
The people in the park are a noisy bunch!

Hannah Coupe (10)
Sibertswold CE Primary School, Dover

Breakfast Time

Pull back the covers
Shuffle, shuffle!
Climb out of bed
Creak, creak!
Walk to the door
Tiptoe, tiptoe!

Go down the stairs
Clank, clank!
Run into the living room
Whoosh, whoosh!
Hear the bacon sizzling
Crackle, crackle!

Switch on the TV
Beep, beep!
The bacon is ready
Ding, ding!
The baked beans are on
Yeah, yeah!
SpongeBob Square Pants
Woooo-hooo!

Stephanie Homewood (10)
Temple Hill CP School, Dartford

Bess

To my bonnie sweetheart, Bess
You're the best of my sweet
You've got eyes like the stars in the night
They are twinkling so much
Your hair is as black as a knight's shining horse
You shine like a light, bright moon
No one can take you
Or my whip will come like a flash of lightning
The bullet of my gun
Will be like a shotgun.

Tyler Tanner (9)
Temple Hill CP School, Dartford

Apple Crumble

I love apple crumble
I always have it for afters
It's so scrummy

It tastes better with juicy apples
Red or green, I don't care
As long as they're juicy

One evening, my mum and dad went out
My mum and dad were going to dinner
My sleepy grandad was here

He lay asleep
On the sofa
He really is a dozer

I suddenly remembered the apple crumble
I went to the fridge, I opened it
There it was

It was beautiful
My mouth was watering

I got a plate
And a knife
I sliced it

I slipped it on my plate
I said to myself,
'That's not enough'

So I took some more
I couldn't stop
Then there was only once slice left

I ran upstairs
It was delicious
I ran back down

I put my plate in the dishwasher

I was safe
Then my grandad woke up, he said to me,
'Am I allowed some apple crumble?'
'Yes,' I said

I gave him a plate
My mum and dad walked in
They saw Grandad with the crumble

They were shocked
Plus angry

I felt guilty
Then I admitted it
I said I was sorry

I wasn't allowed apple crumble for a month.

Alfie Day (9)
Temple Hill CP School, Dartford

At The Football Stadium

People walking down the stairs
Stomp, stomp!
People chanting
Raa, raa!
They score a goal
Boo! Boo!
We score a goal
Yeah! Yeah!
Whistle blows
Whistle, whistle!
Coach shouting
Raa, raa!
We score a goal
Yeah! Yeah!
Whistle blows
Whistle, whistle!
We are cheering
Raa! Raa!
They're crying
Boo-hoo!

Harry Ring (10)
Temple Hill CP School, Dartford

Pizza

One day, me and my cousin and my friends
Went to Pizza Hut
Some of them were Harry, Paige and Alfie and Ope and Juniour,
We had fun
It was the best day of my life.
At the end, my mum bought pizza to take home
It was really cheesy with pepperoni, my favourite
At night, when my mum was asleep, I went downstairs
My mum closed the fridge, thinking someone would take it
When you open our fridge, it makes a loud noise
So I opened it quietly
It looked delicious, *mmm-hmm*
I licked my lips and said, 'Wow! That was good!'

William Azeza (10)
Temple Hill CP School, Dartford

Lunchtime

Ring, ring!
Lunchtime is here
Stomp, stomp!
Children running
Screech, screech!
Chairs scraping
Munch, munch!
Eating sandwiches
Waa! Waa!
People shouting
Crunch, crunch!
People munching
Ring, ring!
No more lunchtime for *play!*

Billy Troke (10)
Temple Hill CP School, Dartford

Bunny Trouble

I bought a brown bunny
I made a small house
For my brown bunny

One night
I left my brown bunny
In a small cage

Then the brown bunny
Got out
And ate all the veg!
Crunch! Crunch!

Mum awoke
Saw the veg was gone
Oh no! oh no!

Looked in bunny's cage
And saw the tops
Of her veg

Mum locked
The bunny
In its small cage

Mum didn't
Let the bunny
Out!

One night
There was
A wind

And it blew
The brown bunny away
In the morning

I cried
So they bought me another
Brown bunny!

Laura Maxwell (9)
Temple Hill CP School, Dartford

Dairy Milk

I love it
It melts in my mouth
I love the bubbly one

I just couldn't wait
I had to save up my money
I kept it away from my sister
Obviously!

Then I had it
Had it in my hand
But where to hide it?
I can just smell it now

I hid it under my pillow
Oh, I couldn't wait
I went to have my dinner
I came back to eat my chocolate

Argh!
No! It was gone
No! All my dreams!

Argh!
Where could it be?

I had to find out who it was
I had to
I just had to

I crept downstairs
Those creaking stairs
Then

Argh!
No! My own little baby sister
Eating my chocolate
The thief!

I hate her
I just hate her
Nicking my chocolate
Nooooooo!

I had an idea
I'd get it back in the night
And gobble the rest up
Yes, yes, yes!

Then I'd put a worm in her hand
And she'd eat it in the morning
Yes, yes, yes!

Down the stairs
Creak, creak
Get the chocolate

I got it
I put the worm in her mouth then

Chew, chew, chew
Eewwww!
She ate a worm
Eewwww!

Finally, my chocolate
Nooooooo!
It was all gone
Nooooooo!

No! I'd have to buy another one
Oh no!

Shannon Burkley (10)
Temple Hill CP School, Dartford

Me And My Chocolate Bar

When I was little
I loved chocolate

I used to have one
Every day
I would say,
'Can I have a chocolate bar?'

And my mum
Would say, 'Yes'

One night, I was in my bed
When I decided to go
And have a little nibble
Mmmmm!

So I crept down
The creaky stairs
And went into the smelly kitchen

I opened the cupboard
And pulled out
My big, blue box

Then I opened it
I pulled out
A chocolate bar

I started to eat
Mmmmm!
Nice

After I had finished
I closed my box
And the cupboard

I went out
Of the smelly kitchen
And shut the door

I went back up
The creaky stairs
And into

My rattly bed
And off to sleep
Zzzzzzz!

Orla Taylor (9)
Temple Hill CP School, Dartford

The Classroom

Everybody taking off their coats
Zip, zip!
Coming into the classroom
Stomp, stomp!
Problems from the playground
'Miss! Miss!'
Sitting on the carpet
Ssh! Ssh!
Calling out
Oi! Oi!
Starting the lesson
'Oh man!'
The clock is going by
Tick-tock!
Someone's got a paper cut
Ouch! Ouch!
Take him to the hospital
No! no!
Look, now he's crying
Boo-hoo!
Don't worry, it's almost home time
Hooray, hooray!
The bell goes
Ding, ding, ding!

Liam Ward (10)
Temple Hill CP School, Dartford

Curry

I like curry
I love curry
My brother does too
My teacher likes curry
Curry is the best dinner, ever

I went to school one day
I smelt the lovely, spicy curry
That the dinner ladies were cooking
I said to the teacher,
'Can I go to the toilet?'
'Yes,' she replied.

So I crept to the canteen
Up to the 'Staff Only' door
And saw the curry lying there
In a big, shiny pot
I crept over and . . .

I slurped it into my mouth
I slurped it and some more
Soon it was gone
The dinner lady came
My curry

I will get every one,
'Was it you?' she said,
'No'
'Was'
'No, it was me, Miss.'

Callum Smith (9)
Temple Hill CP School, Dartford

Swimming

I love swimming
My friend loves swimming
We love it so much
We'll do anything to go

My friend knocked on my door one morning
And said, 'Do you want to come swimming?'
I said, 'Yes, OK then'
So did my mum

So I got my Bratz swimming cossie
And set off

When we got there
We got changed into our cossies
Then we got into the warm pool

I dived in
Then I went down the slide
The lifeguard said, 'No, you can't go on, you're too small'
But I didn't care

I know I was very bad
I mean a bad girl
The plan was very bad
I got thrown out
But I didn't care!

Rachel Massen (9)
Temple Hill CP School, Dartford

In The Cafeteria

Children coming in
Yeah! Yeah! Yeah!
Soup pouring on plates
Slurp, slurp, slurp!
Children talking
Chit-chat, chit-chat!
Head teacher comes in
Clap, clap, clap!
Plates dropping down
Bang, bang, bang!
Spoons in the sink
Crash, crash, crash!
Bell going
Ding-a-ling-a-ling!

Cynthia Ndungu (9)
Temple Hill CP School, Dartford

Kangaroos On The Booze

Kangaroos like their booze
It makes them jump so high
They'll have to be more careful
Or they'll punch a hole in the sky!

Jevan Rowe (9)
Whitstable Endowed CE (A) Junior School, Whitstable

My Cat

My cat loves to eat
My cat loves to sleep
My cat loves to fall over the wall!

Maddy Perry (9)
Whitstable Endowed CE (A) Junior School, Whitstable

The Alien

One day, an alien came to tea
Then it came in and said, 'Fonnodree'
I asked him if he'd want a cake
But my mum said, 'For goodness sake!
Can you get that ugly thing
Out into the rubbish bin!
Get that thing out of my house
It's even worse than a mouse!'
So I chucked him out onto the street
Then he slobbered away on its ugly feet
So the alien went on its way
It might come back another day!

Richard Rowland (9)
Whitstable Endowed CE (A) Junior School, Whitstable

Luke

Luke liked running around the room
Luke liked jumping on the bed
Luke liked splashing in the basin
What do you think his mother said?

Oh
Do stop running around the room
Do stop jumping on the bed
Do stop splashing in the basin
Let's go walk the dog instead!

So
Luke went running around the park
Luke went jumping off the log
Luke went splashing in the puddles
So did his mother and the dog!

William Goldsworthy (9)
Whitstable Endowed CE (A) Junior School, Whitstable

Fantastic Dyspraxic

Dyspraxic, dyspraxic,
People say I'm not fantastic.

Concentration all over the nation
Except one little part,
Yes, it's me, that little pea
And that's one bad thing for a start.

People say I'm a fidget
And I can't stay still on a rock
And that's two times
I've been mocked.

But I'm very good at cooking
And how am I looking
And I've got very good sight
And at least that's two things right.

I'm very clumsy
And spill things dumbly
But at least it makes me funny.

So I may be dyspraxic
But I'm fantastic
And the rest are just a racket.

Joseph Thundow (10)
Whitstable Endowed CE (A) Junior School, Whitstable

My Seaside Town

The sea is fun
The sky is great
It makes me want
To stay up late

The sky is blue
The sea is green
It's even better
Than I have seen

Boats and yachts
I hop on
To the place
Where I belong

It all is great
So as it seems
But I can't swim
So they're just dreams.

Michael Thundow (10)
Whitstable Endowed CE (A) Junior School, Whitstable

Fishes In The Sea

I love fishes swimming in the sea
Once, I was swimming in the sea
When I saw a fish around my knee
And then he swam off with a flick of his tail
Off with the current he goes.

Oliver Ingham (9)
Whitstable Endowed CE (A) Junior School, Whitstable

Winter Weather

W hen it's winter weather, snow's as light as a feather
I t lays down softly, that calls for a cup of coffee
N ever mind, the kettle's broken but I've got words to be spoken
T he words are beautiful black birds
E very bird I saw was singing by the white blanket of snow
R arely I have this experience but it was really nice

W hen the day's over I will be sad
E ven though I've had fun through the day
A fter tea I watch the white snow fade away
T hough I know it will be back some day
H owever I don't like snow for long, I'll be partly glad when it's gone
E very day I'll hope and pray everyone's happy in the same way
R ough ice stays, so I will go.

Lauren Abbott (10)
Whitstable Endowed CE (A) Junior School, Whitstable

Cat

The mouse and the house
There was a cat
Who sat on a mat
He saw a mouse
Who knocked down his house
His mum came back
And screamed out loud,
'Where's my house?'

Hollie Pring (9)
Whitstable Endowed CE (A) Junior School, Whitstable

All About Me

I'm as tall as a tree, with knobbly knees,
I'm as big as a bee, well lucky me,
I like to yawn at the start of dawn,
Well, look at me, what else can I be?

I like to eat chips with my juicy lips,
I like to sing when we're in the bling,
I like to swim, in the blowing wind,
Look at me, what else can I be?

I laugh all the time, boy, this doesn't rhyme,
I bark like a dog, that sat on a log,
I jump like a pea, that was cooked in t'ai chi,
Look at me, what else can I be?

Amber Manning (11)
Whitstable Endowed CE (A) Junior School, Whitstable

Will You Eat Off A Dish?

I have a poem, it won't take long,
But if you don't like it
It will start to pong
I have a fish who won't eat off a dish
I don't know why he just won't eat pie
I give him peas
Then he starts to wheeze
He won't make a wish without his dish.

Maddy Temple (9)
Whitstable Endowed CE (A) Junior School, Whitstable

Maths

Maths is fun,
Maths is cool,
You think I'm insane,
But I'll show you.

Maths takes a brain,
Which nobody's got,
Maths isn't lame,
No, really, it's not.

Maths is great,
Maths is clever,
Maths is a mate,
So don't be late.

Maths is for boys,
As literacy's for girls,
Maths is like some toys,
That are only for the big boys.

Maths uses computers,
Although they're very small,
They fit in my palm,
But I'm not very tall.

I like maths,
I like numbers,
I like sums,
That use big numbers.

Maths is the best,
It's better than the rest,
Maths doesn't drool,
It rules!

Andy Beaumont (10)
Whitstable Endowed CE (A) Junior School, Whitstable

Snow Day

There it lay in the afternoon,
All spread out as white as the moon,
Looking so harmless where it lay,
It never knew it was getting in the way,
Cars were sliding everywhere,
People were trampling anywhere.

A snowball fight broke out at school,
The poor snow was looking like a pool,
It soon turned into mud and slush,
Then the teachers told us to hush,
Everything was so quiet from then,
But I have a plan to snowball the men.

Katie Horton (11)
Whitstable Endowed CE (A) Junior School, Whitstable

Snowfall

S now is fun
N otice gritters, what! Don't grit
O ver all, snow is cool
W ish it would lay longer
F inally evaporates in the air
A lmost gone
L ook at me in the snow
L et it snow, let it grow.

Katy Terrell (11)
Whitstable Endowed CE (A) Junior School, Whitstable

Football

Football is great
I play with my best mate

If I get the ball
I pass it to Paul

I make a route
Then I shoot

It goes in
I'm always screaming

Goal!

Eleanor Dwyers (10)
Whitstable Endowed CE (A) Junior School, Whitstable

Without You

Without you, I'm like . . .
A question mark without a question
A Chanzard without a flame
A match without any players
A pen without any ink
A plane without any wings
A tree without any leaves.

Thomas Dwyer (9)
Yerbury Primary School, London

Young Writers Information

We hope you have enjoyed reading this book - and that you will continue to enjoy it in the coming years.

If you like reading and writing poetry drop us a line, or give us a call, and we'll send you a free information pack.

Alternatively if you would like to order further copies of this book or any of our other titles, then please give us a call or log onto our website at www.youngwriters.co.uk

**Young Writers Information
Remus House
Coltsfoot Drive
Peterborough
PE2 9JX**

(01733) 890066